INTEGRATING COMPUTERS IN YOUR CLASSROOM

EARLY CHILDHOOD

BY PETER DUBLIN, HARVEY PRESSMAN,
EILEEN BARNETT and EVELYN J. WOLDMAN

HarperCollins*CollegePublishers*

This book was developed and produced by Intentional Educations, Inc. of Watertown, Massachusetts. Intentional Educations is one of the country's foremost developers of educational materials, both books and software. We wish to thank the following people for their contribution to this book:

Interior book design:
    Dee Nee Reiten-Skipper
Cover design and mechanicals:
    Sylvia Frezzolini
Cover illustrations:
    Marti Shohet
Interior cartoons:
    Larry Butler
Part I interior illustrations:
    Cheryl Kirk Noll
Part II interior illustrations:
    Elizabeth Manicatide
Editorial assistance:
    Susan Christie Woodward
    Andrea Infantino
    Melissa Willson
Typesetting:
    Peter Dublin

$L B$
1028.5
$E2$
1994

Copyright © 1994 Intentional Educations, Inc.

ISBN: 0-06-501894-X

94 95 96 97 9 8 7 6 5 4 3 2 1

Contents

PREFACE

The computer will play an important part in schools if it plays an important part in classrooms. The classroom remains the cornerstone of education in schools, so for computers to be important in schools, they must be important in classrooms. That is the reason this book is entitled "Integrating Computers in Your Classroom." That is the reason we make precious little mention of Computer Labs or Media Centers.

Computers have been knocking on the doors of education for over thirty years. Through the 1970's, time-sharing, mainframes, and programmed instruction dominated computer activity in the schools. From the end of the 1970's through the 1980's, the personal computer led the so-called "computer revolution" in the schools. Now, in the 1990's, many are wondering whether this "revolution" might have passed us by.

We believe the fundamental changes in education are still ahead of us, and that computers can play an important role in helping to shape those changes. The changes, however are not likely to be primarily technological. The changes we envision involve changing classrooms into effective educational environments for many more of the children who attend them. If the computer is to have any significant impact on education, it will be as part of broader pedagogical changes that make classrooms more engaging and exciting environments able to respond to a broader variety of learning differences in the students who inhabit them.

And how is this to happen? The key word for us is: "integration." This book is intended to make it easier and more valuable for you to integrate computers into the daily instruction that takes place in your classroom. The classroom is at the center of the school, the classroom teacher is at the center of the classroom, and this book is for you, the classroom teacher.

All authors have a particular audience in mind for their books. For us, the "you" for whom this book is intended is the "beginning" teacher. But we believe that there are two kinds of beginners in this field. On the one hand, we intend this book for beginners who have never been classroom teachers before. If you are taking a course as part of your preparation for becoming a teacher, you fit into this category. On the other hand, we intend this book to be very useful to experienced teachers who are novice computer-using teachers. If you are currently teaching, and are reading this book because you have a computer in your room that you know you aren't getting the most out of, you fit into this category. So, if you are either of these kinds of beginners, you have come to the right book. We talk in plain language, not in bits and bytes. We talk more pedagogy than we talk technology. And we include a myriad of practical, easy-to-implement activities that you can immediately apply in your classroom, many of which do not even assume a specific piece of software.

Integrating Computers in Your Classroom is part of an eight-book series. In future years, we hope the success of these initial titles will enable us to add even more titles. Each book is designed to help teachers at specific grade levels integrate computers in their on-going classroom practice. Although you are reading just one of these books, we want you to know that the series includes:

Integrating Computers in Your Classroom: Early Childhood,
Integrating Computers in Your Classroom: Elementary Language Arts,
Integrating Computers in Your Classroom: Elementary Math,
Integrating Computers in Your Classroom: Elementary Science,
Integrating Computers in Your Classroom: Elementary Grades,
Integrating Computers in Your Classroom: Middle & Secondary English,
Integrating Computers in Your Classroom: Middle & Secondary Math, and
Integrating Computers in Your Classroom: Middle & Secondary Science

The series nature of *Integrating Computers in Your Classroom* means a number of things. First, it means that all of the books in the series share certain commonalities. All the books share a common structure, comprised of essays, case studies, classroom activities, and bundled software.

Second, the series nature enables us to focus each book on an appropriately narrow area. This is especially true for the practical classroom activities which comprise Part II of each book. The result is that you will find a substantial number of practical activities which you can use in your classroom.

Part I: Essays and Case Studies

Each book in this series includes eighteen short essays, grouped into five chapters. Each essay is short, to the point, and simply stated. Each essay raises a single issue. All of them are intended to raise general issues, not issues specific to a particular content area or grade level. That is why, in fact, these essays appear in each of the books in the series.

The open-ended and occasionally irreverent questions that start off each essay may not all seem at first (or even second) glance to be immediately relevant to the specific material at hand. We include them because we want to encourage you to take a questioning attitude to what you are reading, as well as to what is currently going on with computers and schools. We believe that books for teachers, like software for students, are sometimes better when they occasionally raise questions without answering every single one of them, while providing you with additional resources with which to grapple with the questions.

Part I is the closest we get to theory. The essays lay out a framework for thinking about the integration of computers into ordinary classrooms. They reflect a set of values, both pedagogical and social/political. We hope they will provide a context that will help you utilize the more practical activities throughout the back half of the book more thoughtfully.

Part I is also practical. Therefore, we have concluded each chapter with a case study. The case studies illustrate practical implementation of at least one of the essays in that chapter. Unlike the essays–which raise general issues and are the same throughout all the books in the series–the case studies are examples of practical implementation. They are different for each book in the series and have been selected to illustrate specific examples of computer integration appropriate to the age-range and subject matter of each book.

Part II: Practical Classroom Activities

The back half of this book is comprised exclusively of practical classroom activities. In one sense, they are similar to the case studies, in that they illustrate examples of practical implementation. They are fundamentally different, however, from the case studies. A case study works well if it gives you a concrete sense of successful strategies that teachers can use to incorporate computer technology in their everyday classroom life. An activity works well if you can immediately put it to use.

We are also convinced that one of the major faults with the presentation of classroom activities in most education texts is the one-dimensional nature of that presentation. As a result, we utilize four different and distinct formats in presenting the activities at the back of these books:

Lesson Plan

This is the format most familiar to most teachers. It includes a series of categories (teacher preparation, materials needed, procedures, follow-up, and so forth) which structure the information. The Lesson Plan is the category which includes step-by-step instructions or procedures. We utilize this format when it is critical to know these detailed procedures.

Unit Plan

The Lesson Plan format is designed to describe a lesson that takes place over one or two days. The Unit Plan format is designed to describe a series of activities that take place over time, often a week or more. Each Unit Plan divides its materials into a small number of categories, categories which vary from unit plan to unit plan.

Up Front

We utilize two narrative formats to describe activities. The first of these is a first person account. In this "Up Front" format, the teacher doing the activity describes that activity. All the information you need to implement the activity is still included, but in a different, more personal style, with a focus on the reasons why a teacher has done certain things. Each Up Front account concludes with a set of Teacher Tips, designed to fill in some gaps left out of the narrative.

From the Sidelines

This is the second of the two narrative forms: the third person account. In From the Sidelines, an observer in the classroom describes what is happening. We also have an observer with a real perspective: another teacher, a principal, a newspaper reporter, a school board member, an interested parent, and so forth. Each account concludes with a Teacher's Response, where the teacher doing the activity can respond to what the observer has written. Some Teacher Responses are humorous, some argumentative, and often the teacher explains his or her reasons for doing what he or she did.

The classroom activities are not clustered separately into these five categories. We have purposely mixed up the activities to create some variety in what you are reading and to make it more enjoyable for you to "shop" through the various kinds of activities available.

Bundled Software

Integrating Computers in Your Classroom is dedicated to helping you integrate the use of computers in your own classroom, as well as other aspects of your professional life. As a result, we have bundled with this book a piece of *Lesson Planner* software.

The *Lesson Planner* software functions in two important ways. First, it functions as a tutorial. There is a series of on-screen tutorials–called Guides–designed to walk you through the process of preparing a lesson plan. The Guides help you look at the sources for lesson plans, the importance of a planning and brainstorming stage, the need to get ideas on screen and into a file, the ways in which those initial ideas can be organized and structured, and so forth. The software also includes Practice Files which provide a number of lesson plan templates. All of these pedagogical components are included with an easy-to-use word processor, which you use to write your lesson plans.

At some point, of course, you will no longer need the tutorial and the program turns into a tool which you can use to write your lesson plans. The software includes an on-line database of twenty activities. You can search through this database (for all the spreadsheet activities) or simply browse through the activities. When you find one around which you want to build a lesson plan, you can electronically copy it into your word processing file.

At the same time, the *Lesson Planner* software allows you to add your own activities. You can use the software as a way to store your best activity ideas, because the database nature of the program allows for both easy storage and easy retrieval. And you will have the power of the software to build lesson plans around your own favorite activities while becoming more comfortable with using computers and more aware of their power and utility within your classroom.

About This Book

The 1991 Carnegie Foundation Report, *Ready to Learn: A Mandate for the Nation,* found that at least 35% of America's kindergarten students are not well prepared for school. Integrating computers into early childhood programs can contribute to solving this problem, as much by raising young children's feelings of control over the materials they are trying to master as by teaching any particular set of skills like eye/hand coordination. Children who learn to use computers at an early age can get a noticeable boost to their self-esteem, and, if they are encouraged to work with others at the computer, seem to increase their communication skills.

A statement from the U.S. Department of Education suggests another important reason for integrating computers in early childhood programs: "... evidence indicates that the use of software and computer assisted media and materials based on sound developmental and educational principles has the potential to provide young children early opportunities and experiences in thinking and problem solving strategies that are *the foundation and building blocks that enable future learning.*" The statement also emphasizes the potential "development and learning gains by preschoolers as a result of technology use," and the urgent national need to demonstrate how to take advantage of them. Evidence exists that preschoolers who take advantage of current technologies become *better* problem solvers, and that, contrary to popular myth, computers help stimulate, rather than deter, social interaction among preschoolers. Researchers have found evidence that computers stimulate the social interaction of young children to the benefit of their problem solving, and that children who use computers become both more persistent and effective at solving problems.

Why? Perhaps because figuring out how to use a computer is itself a challenging problem-solving task. Figuring out to use a particular piece of software may be another. If the software is as good as the material cited in Part Two of this book, moreover, it can help young children become better problem-solvers because they get the chance to manipulate open-ended programs like *KidPix* and *Millie's Math House* in a way that increases the choices and options in their early learning, while still taking into account the developmental stages they are growing through.

It is not necessary to stray from the most valued precepts of developmental learning in order to use the best available technology tools. We hope that you, after using this book, will find it easier to conceive of ways to use computers for a wide variety of such purposes, including:

- finding "another way" to help struggling students master code breaking and reading fluency skills,
- helping students "concretize" early math and science concepts,
- stimulating task-related verbal communication that supports the development of oral expression.
- providing "reluctant" writers with a way to succeed at writing,

PART I

"This book focuses on the practical ways that computers can create a significant, positive impact on thousands of classrooms.

◆ It is not about using computers to replace teachers.
◆ It is not about using computers in laboratory situations."

First Principles

Dear Dr. DeLeet:

I have been teaching for twelve years and I am just now getting around to using computers in my classroom (the high school bought new Macs, and sent down these old Apple IIs to our middle school). My problem is that now my principal seems to expect me to perform miracles with these machines. I don't get it. It was hard enough to find the time to meet all the other new "mandates" that have been forced down our throats in the last few years. How am I supposed to know how to use these things? Where will I get the time to learn? Why is this so important, anyway?

A Fed-up Veteran

CHAPTER 1

Computers Within Classrooms

- **What if they gave a revolution and no one came?**
- **What kind of revolution is this, anyway?**
- **Is this steak, or just sizzle?**

The primary teachers in a rural school in Tennessee are gathered together for an afternoon in-service session on "Making More Effective Use of Our Computer Resources." The trainer hands the teachers sheets of paper asking them to choose their "top two" ways to complete the following sentence:

MORE TEACHERS WILL USE COMPUTERS WHEN:

(a) they learn how to use them to develop higher order thinking skills;

(b) they learn how to use them to promote learning by doing;

(c) they learn how to use them to respond to student differences in learning styles;

(d) they learn how to use them to encourage cooperative learning;

(e) they learn how to use them to give students a chance to practice, practice, practice things like vocabulary, spelling, and arithmetic facts;

(f) they learn how to use them to help students improve their scores on standardized basic skill exams;

(g) they learn how to use them to promote learning by teaching.

[See the end of this essay for their top two choices. What do you think they were?]

America's schools have been caught up in the "computer revolution" for at least fifteen years. So, why is there a growing sense that this revolution has fizzled? Why do so many experts say that the impact of 18-20 billion dollars worth of technology investments on the basic operation of most classrooms is "practically nil?" What kind of revolution is this, anyway?

The Failed Revolution

One clue to this mystery involves the simple question: Where? We know that most school learning still takes place inside ordinary, "self-contained" classrooms. So whether most children develop adequate skills depends on what happens *within* these classrooms. There is also evidence that computers can provide valuable classroom support in teaching subjects that are at the core of the curriculum. Yet study after study shows that schools use computers primarily as drill and practice machines, or as "toys" offering rewards for good behavior. And far too often, even these uninspiring interventions occur outside the boundaries of the regular classroom, in laboratories, media centers, and other ill-named "sanctuaries."

History may offer another clue to the lost revolution. Computers began showing up in schools in the 1950's and 1960's, accompanied by rumblings of impending revolution. These new marvels first appeared in school offices and computer labs. They were networked, utilized time-sharing on mainframes over modems, and were run by the computer expert. They fizzled. In the late 1970's and early 1980's, "personal" computers entered the schools with even greater fanfare. These were simpler machines which individual teachers and their students could use within their own classrooms, buying individual pieces of software to support the core activity of the classroom. By the late 1980's, however, personal computers had rediscovered their mainframe roots; and more and more drifted away to computer labs and central offices. Once again they were networked, distanced from teachers, and run by network specialists.

What This Book is NOT

This book focuses on the practical ways that computers can create a significant, positive impact on thousands of classrooms.

- ◆ It is not about marginalizing the use of computers in schools, nor about using computers for administrative purposes, by either administrators or teachers.
- ◆ It is not about using computers as the electronic equivalent of the Friday afternoon movie, to keep kids quiet for a couple of hours.
- ◆ It is not about using computers as drill-and-practice machines.
- ◆ It is not about using computers to replace teachers.
- ◆ It is not about teaching computer literacy.
- ◆ It is not about using the computer to support hardware manufacturers' search for new markets.
- ◆ It is not about using computers as a reward. It is not about letting students play games after successfully completing "real" work.
- ◆ It is not about using computers in laboratory situations.

What This Book IS

This book is about using computers inside real classrooms. This book is fundamentally a practical book. If you are training to be a teacher, it will help you see the computer as an invaluable tool in your future profession. If you are already a teacher, it will help you get beyond the fear of the computer as an esoteric device useful only to those who know its innards. This is a book to read and enjoy, but it is even more a book for you to put to practical use.

◆   It is about integrating computers in your classroom. It is about helping you use whatever computer resources are available to you.

◆   It is about helping you see the connection between educational software and the other curriculum materials you utilize.
◆   It is about tying computer use to major curriculum goals. It is about supporting your core efforts within your classroom with effective and innovative educational software.
◆   It is about using the computer as a tool to promote student learning within the regular curriculum. It is about using the computer as a tool to help your students learn about anything and everything. It is about using software "productivity tools" to learn about all school subjects.

◆　It is about using computers in cooperative and innovative ways and
supporting the varied learning styles of all your students.
◆　It is about new ways to use computers to help your weaker students
gain basic skills.

The essays which make up most of Part I provide an intellectual context
within which to practice sensible computer integration. Interspersed among
these essays are specific case studies that exemplify actual ways in which people
are practicing what this book preaches. Part II is probably the most practical
part of this book. It is full of classroom activities, described from various points
of view (teachers, parents, students, principals, etc.) And the software
"bundled" with the book has been designed as a convenient tool to help you
write lesson plans and save lesson ideas for future reference.

[The teachers in Tennessee chose (c) how to respond to learning styles
differences and (f) how to help students improve their scores on standardized
basic skill exams, as their top two goals.

What We Emphasize and Why

- **Should kids be required to wear white coats in computer labs?**
- **Are productivity tools capitalist tools?**
- **Are some computers more equal than others?**

*A computer coordinator in a large Santa Monica elementary school is describing her
frustration at the way classroom teachers in her system use computers when they finally get
around to "allowing" them within the hallowed walls of their classrooms. "Most teachers," she reports, "think of computers as extras, not tools of their trade. The kind of thing
I hear them say to their students most often is: 'If you finish your WORK, I'll let you go to
the computer corner and PLAY with Millie's Math House.'"*

What computers can do is impressive; what schools use computers for is
often trivial. Even schools that try to use computers to achieve key instructional
goals still usually try to do it by pulling students out of regular classrooms into a
segregated environment. The computer becomes a subject rather than a tool,
and most teachers are allowed to avoid confronting the need to learn how to
put this new "tool of their trade" to practical use. This basic situation has
shaped the priorities and emphases of this book.

Computers Within Classrooms

The classroom teacher is still the one who delivers the core learning that takes place in schools. To locate computers outside of the classroom–the central context of the school–trivializes computers and their potential for change. Computer labs are easy and (supposedly) cost-effective ways to put computers in schools, which may be why administrators and hardware manufacturers gravitate towards them. Computer labs are not *inherently* irrelevant, but they minimize, encapsulate, thus impeding the computer from playing a more central role in the educational process you, as the classroom teacher, are responsible for mediating. Computer labs also maintain the "mystery" of the common ordinary computer–which needs to be demystified in most schools–and can keep instructional and pedagogical decisions in the hands of people whose primary skills are technological rather than educational. For all these reasons, this book emphasizes integrating computers in your classroom.

Classrooms With 1-3 Computers

There is no good reason to ponder the ideal number of computers in a single classroom. The number of computers in your classroom will probably not, in the near future (if ever), be dictated by reason; the number will be dictated by budgetary realities. Those realities indicate that you can expect to have between one and three computers...at most. Since this book is designed to help you deal with the most likely practical realities you will confront within your classroom, most of the "What Do I Do Monday Morning" activities at the back of this book assume that you will have a limited number of computers in your classroom.

Cooperative Learning

One of the most common misconceptions about computers is that they are ideal instruments for *individual* learning. Clearly, that use of computers may sometimes be legitimate in theory, and is common in practice. But you know that solo learning is often not the most appropriate or effective pedagogical strategy. Too often computers are used to "atomize" and isolate students from each other. Cooperative learning has become a central pedagogy in many classrooms, for its instructional, social, and motivational benefits. The computer may well prove far more effective in cooperative learning settings than in individualized learning situations. The cooperative approach both humanizes the computer and integrates its use into common and important educational practice. That is why we place such an emphasis on using the computer in the context of cooperative learning experiences.

Accommodating Diversity

Why does this book emphasize the computer as an asset to meeting the needs of diverse students? A clear problem in contemporary American education is that it too rarely acknowledges, fosters, and takes advantage of the diversity with which it is increasingly confronted. Some educators even blame diversity for their own failures, instead of looking to diversity as a springboard for increasing their success.

Computers can provide you with a rich variety of teaching strategies, accommodating to widely divergent learning styles, multiple intelligences, and special learning needs within your classroom. The atmosphere in today's classroom often reinforces the tendency to teach to the linguistic, logical-mathematical, and intrapersonal learner and virtually ignore the other "intelligences" that students possess. This tendency misses the chance to validate and develop all the intelligences of all children and fails to take advantage of the likelihood that the more ways a subject is presented, the better that subject is learned. The reason for extending computer activities to reach all the intelligences is very simple: you can better utilize the match between the resources you have, the way you use them, and the dominant intelligences of your students.

In the hands of a gifted teacher, computers are thus not just tools to accommodate or adapt to ONE other kind of student learner, but to a number of different kinds of learners. With the right software, the computer can become a tool for responding to the needs of students who do better when they can visualize the concrete manifestations of a mathematics operation (as with Ventura's *Hands-On Math* series), or a student who needs more practice in the way to set up the solution to math word problems (*Outnumbered*), or a student with a physical or learning disability who needs shortcuts in keyboarding (Hartley's *My Words*, Don Johnston's *Predict It*), etc. Computers can provide your students who have learning disabilities or physical handicaps entry points to learning and communicating they have never before experienced in schools.

With respect to students with special needs, it is important to note that the student who is fully integrated in the regular classroom can thrive in a number of important ways (academic, social, psychological, etc.) as a result of that integration, and that computers can be effective tools for facilitating the kind of integration that prevents students with special needs from becoming "islands in the mainstream." Such students can be given special roles, for example, in cooperative learning activities around the computer. Giving students with special needs roles as cross-age computer tutors of younger students enables them to gain in self-esteem, and raise their own academic achievement while relearning some skills they may not have completely mastered first time around. Most important, from the point of view of the classroom teacher, the classroom computer can make it easier to deal successfully with the learning differences of students with special needs.

Productivity Tools

Why does this book include so many classroom activities that use spreadsheets, word processors and other productivity tools? In a word–access. Even if your school has a very limited software budget, you can usually obtain productivity tools. Productivity tools can be used effectively for learning activities across the entire curriculum. They can be used easily by students from the elementary grades through high school. And, since such tools are used in real life in a variety of home and job-related contexts, using them in your school for instructional purposes has the added benefit of helping your students learn to use tools they will need in their adult lives.

Thinking Skills

Why does this book place such an emphasis on thinking skills? As our society changes more rapidly and becomes ever more complex, mastering a static body of knowledge becomes less critical than the ability to analyze and process new information about key content areas. Throughout the curriculum, from science and math to language arts and social studies, teachers are beginning to focus on the skills their students need to understand and work with that content. In addition, once students master certain higher order thinking skills, they seem to achieve at higher levels in future grades. The computer may not be a great tool for *acquiring* information, but it is a fantastic resource for utilizing and manipulating information. That is why we place such an emphasis on thinking skills.

What Research Says to the Teacher

- **You can lead a school to software, but you cannot make it compute.**
- **Will the mice play when the sage gets off the stage?**
- **Does software have to be used as a dessert?**

The superintendent has gathered together his "leadership team" to begin discussing the next "five-year plan" for the use of technology in a large California school system. The expert he has brought in starts by displaying a series of quotes taken from the recent research literature on computers and schools. Some of the statements had been altered to reverse their meaning; some were direct quotations from the literature. The teachers were asked to guess which were the "original statements" and which were "fraudulent reversals" of the original. Can you sort out the true findings?

1. *The effects of Computer Based Instruction seem especially clear in studies promoting the development of basic academic skills with pupils who have traditionally been classified as "disadvantaged."*

2. *The most consequential finding in the body of literature regarding IBM's Writing to Read is that its use in the development of writing skills is significantly different from an individual teacher's use of the process approach to writing within a traditional classroom environment.*

3. *A 1990 University of Michigan study reported that children can gain the equivalent of three months of instruction per school year when computers are available to them.*

4. *Students in both the cooperative and the competitive conditions performed lower on an achievement test than did the students in the individualistic [i.e. one-on-one] condition.*

5. *The LOGO computer programming language has been described as an environment in which children will develop problem-solving skills. Unfortunately, much of the research concerned with LOGO and problem-solving has not found such connection.*

The team had trouble sorting out which statements were fraudulent reversals (numbers 2 and 4 above).

Does knowing about the research makes any difference, for policymakers or teachers? Importantly, it does, because the research is pointing in a very clear direction. Unfortunately, it is the road NOT taken by most school systems. What some of the research says to you as a teacher is that you could be using software to get a lot more help achieving important classroom objectives than you may realize from the way computers are presently being used in your school.

How Can Computers Help?

Before most teachers, or principals, are likely to take the time, energy, and effort required to learn about effective uses of computers within classrooms, they need to know whether it is worth it. As Larry Cuban has cogently demonstrated, most teachers will utilize new technologies only to the degree that they believe that these technologies will help them solve problems that *they* define as important. Cuban also suggests that schools usually go through a consistent cyclical pattern in their response to new technologies: (1) exhilaration, (2) scientific credibility, (3) disappointment, and (4) blame. (*Harvard Ed. Review*, 2/89.)

Currently available research and evaluation studies does yet draw definitive conclusions about the ultimate potential of computers as a tool used wisely within the regular classroom. But they do provide tantalizing evidence that in certain areas, the computer has already demonstrated its capacity to provide invaluable support in helping teachers accomplish goals that they themselves define as crucial to their success.

Are Computers Being Used Well?

What does the research say? Presently schools use computers primarily as individualized drill and practice machines, or (occasionally) as extracurricular enrichment tools, not as tools to support basic learning. Students from poorer communities and underachieving students often get less access to computers.

And when they *do* get access, they are too often confined to drill and practice and tutorial activities. (H.J. Becker, *Communications of the ACM*, 1983.)

Another lost opportunity comes because of teachers and administrators who consider computers one-on-one learning devices; the advantages of having students work together around a computer are neglected. Students who do get to work in small groups are rarely taught specific skills and roles for cooperative learning, with the result that many of the major benefits of small group work around the computer are still lost.

Researchers who look at the use of computers in schools are coming to the following conclusions:

1. Although schools have bought lots of computers, most of these machines cannot impact classroom instruction, because they do not end up inside classrooms.

2. When computers do make it into the classroom, they are rarely used in ways that tie in closely with basic instruction, so that they can not be expected to significantly impact that instruction.

3.   Wherever the computers are, their use is marginal to the core of instruction going on in classrooms.
4.   Even when an effort is made to connect computer work to the core curriculum, the connections are often superficial or peripheral.
5.   When computers are integrated into the basic life of the classroom in meaningful ways, they seem to have the power to make a significant difference in the effectiveness of classroom instruction.

Research and Styles of Teaching

A second indicator of the potential of classroom computers involves their use as a part of a broader series of changes designed to help teachers move away from "lectern" styles of teaching to other forms of classroom organization that involve small group learning, peer tutoring, learning stations, cooperative learning, and the like.

Computer-based activities, such as simulations and many tool uses, make small-group problem-solving by students possible. Teachers can manage groups of students, rather than conduct the more typical whole-class activity. As Jan Hawkins and Karen Sheingold point out, managing and supporting such work effectively requires observational skills different from those teachers normally apply, and new intuitions about when and how to intervene in student-based activities, as well as how to monitor the progress of individual students. ("Computers and the Organization of Learning," in Culbertson, *et.al.*, *Microcomputers in Education*, 1986.)

Research and Achievement

A third set of studies relates directly to the use of computers in heterogeneous classrooms in helping underachievers to raise their basic skill levels:

◆   Children on the lower end of achievement scales seem to benefit the most from using computers. (Lillie, *et.al.*, *Computers and Effective Instruction*, 1989.)
◆   Computers can reduce student learning time in many subject areas.
◆   The use of word processing by children as young as third- and fourth-graders can produce striking changes in their attitudes towards writing. (Riel, *Journal of Educational Computing Research*, 1985, p. 317-377.)
◆   Students can learn math skills more quickly and cost effectively when instruction is supplemented by the use of computers than with tradi-

tional instruction. (Center for Advanced Technology in Education, University of Oregon.)

Research and Diversity

One clue to the potential of computers involves their use as a tool for helping teachers accommodate greater diversity in learning abilities and styles within a single classroom. Lynne Outhred points out that use of the word processor results in children writing longer and better stories, with greater willingness to revise their work. In a study in the *Journal of Learning Disabilities* (April, 1989), she reports that children with learning disabilities had fewer spelling errors and increased the length of their written efforts. Holz, using computers to teach basic money-handling skills to trainable mentally handicapped students (ages 7-20), found achievement differences to be statistically significant in favor of those using computers.

Research and Learning

Computers seem able to improve problem-solving skills in a wide variety of situations: e.g., at preschool levels, in conjunction with cooperative learning, for third and fifth graders trying to improve their math concept skills, in conjunction with the use of simulation software. Computers have also been shown to enhance students' motivation to learn and their attitude towards the subject matter, as well as student interaction and the amount of "on-task verbal activity" that occurs among students. Finally, research indicates that the relationship between teacher and student is central to successful computer-mediated education, and that the most "successful" teachers are "orchestrators," who integrate and coordinate computer activities with other means of instruction.

Case Study ▬▬▬▬▬▬▬▬▬▬▬▬▬▬▬▬▬▬▬▬▬▬▬▬▬▬▬▬▬▬▬▬▬▬ ■

The View from the Top

This story describes how Michael Shaw, the director of a
preschool, inadvertently discovered how technology could add a
new dimension to the preschool experience. His story illustrates how
one computer, whose original purpose was administrative support,
spread its influence through many aspects of the preschool environment. Michael was able to:
- capture the interest and imagination of the children;
- energize the entire school and parent community;
- reduce and simplify his administrative tasks.

As the director of a large Early Childhood Center, Michael
Shaw was burdened with an overwhelming amount of administrative
paperwork. Whether it was forms for the state or town, notices and
newsletters to parents, bookkeeping chores, activity sheets, handouts or classroom decorations, he found that he constantly was
faced with paper tasks which took up too much time.

Early in the year, Michael attended an Early Childhood
Conference sponsored by the State Department of Education. As
he browsed through the conference program, a workshop entitled
"Ten Ways to Get Out From Under Your Paperwork" jumped out at
him. "Hmm," he thought, "that sounds perfect for me." When he
entered the room, however, it was filled with computers. Were they
kidding? He hated anything mechanical. Computers? Him?
Impossible. It was too late, though. He was already in the room and
too embarrassed to turn around and walk out.

Two hours later, at the end of the session, he was beginning to
change his mind. He had a fistful of handouts with simple ideas
and instructions on how to get started. The only thing he needed
was a computer, but he had no idea where one would come from.
The Center certainly didn't have a slush fund. They didn't even
have enough money to buy ice cream at the end of the school year.

Then he remembered that many of the parents worked in the
technology industry, and he decided to ask them to help. Wonder of
wonders, he got what he asked for. It wasn't the newest machine

on the market, but it had what he needed. He spent the time necessary to learn how to use the computer and, in no time at all, he was ready to go it alone. He could see that the computer was the perfect tool. He made a list of all the paper work he found overwhelming and prioritized it. Then he decided to tackle one thing at a time, starting with something very easy and fun.

Halloween was just around the corner and his teachers were requesting some fresh wall decorations. On a whim, he rolled the computer and printer into one of the classrooms. Using one of the software packages shown at the conference and a color ribbon, he began to design and print a banner sporting witches, pumpkins and ghosts. It was really fun. Before he knew it, there was a group of children and the teacher clustered around him, totally engrossed in what he was doing. Soon the kids were making suggestions, choosing designs and pictures and wanting "to try" the computer. They were delighted with the large poster decorations and banners that came rolling off the printer. He decided, that from then on, the children and their teachers would take turns creating the decorations for the school. Everyone was so excited about it, they had to draw straws to see which classroom would be in charge of decorations.

With this success under his belt, Michael was ready to tackle something a bit more difficult–a newsletter. The software he chose was designed to be used by elementary school students. It was so easy, he was able to produce a rough draft in a very short time. He added a picture and some neat graphics (included in the software) and had the spiffiest newsletter that had ever come out of his office. Parents and teachers noticed the difference and commented appreciatively on its content and appearance. Michael was surprised at how quickly the computer was becoming an integral part in the operation of the preschool.

Over the course of the year, Michael learned how to use spreadsheet software to help with daily school budget records. Students used printing and drawing programs and submitted their drawings for inclusion in the school newsletter. Teachers wrote personalized status reports to parents and created their own classroom activity sheets. Parents began to borrow software to try at home. All this because of one small computer. What had started as a practical approach to alleviating an administrative burden had become an exciting exploration in computer learning.   ▬■

"COMPUTERS CAN BE VERY POWERFUL TOOOOLS!"

"Hardware and software each provide their problems for teachers, but the two components are different, with different solutions to their problems."

The Resources at Hand

Dear Dr. DeLeet:

   I am in my last year of graduate school here at the Michigan State Department Of Sociology (MS-DOS), with a minor in Education and just received word that my application to teach sixth grade next year here in inner-city Glancing has been accepted. My problem is that they have told me that my sixth grade class will have access to only two Apple IIE's that sit outside in the corridor, and I've used only IBM's to write my papers and stuff here at MS-DOS. (I did get an A- in my computer literacy course, but I still don't think I know much about using these things with kids.) My question is: Will it be worth my while to spend the time to learn how to use these old machines in my hectic first year of teaching?

A Fearful Rookie

CHAPTER **2**

Getting Started

- **Begin what is difficult where it is easy?**
- **Where have all the old tools gone?**
- **Is computer illiteracy a badge of honor?**

Anita Stewert could not believe what was happening to her. She had been teaching for 28 years, and she considered herself an excellent teacher. And now her principal was asking her–demanding, it seemed–to integrate computers into her kindergarten classroom. She did not know a thing about them; in fact, she had never used a computer herself in her life. Never felt the need, and did not feel it now.

"I don't even know if I approve of computers," she told the principal. "I'm afraid they will make my classroom too impersonal. From everything I hear, they're difficult to use, foreboding, and unforgiving. Do not even bother pretending that they are teacher-friendly, hassle-free aids. As far as I can tell, computers have earned their bad reputation."

Starting to use computers inside a classroom where they have not been used before is not an easy task. Consciously, semi-consciously, sometimes even subconsciously, you may be mulling over some of these questions: Do I really have time for this? Is it worth the effort? How am I going to manage the logistics? Will it upset my existing classroom dynamics in some unexpected way? Is it possible to truly *integrate* these machines? Where to begin?

In addition, you may not know your way around computers; you may not know whether you really like them or approve of them; and you may not even feel comfortable expressing your ambivalence, or even admitting it to yourself. And computers have sometimes earned a bad reputation. They *can* sometimes be difficult to use, and unforgiving, while all the while someone in authority is pretending they are these teacher-friendly, hassle-free "aids." What is needed are some easier ways of integrating computers into classrooms, and some straight talk about the very real barriers that still exist.

This book is for teachers who are ready to take advantage of a newly available tool to make classroom teaching better–and more fun–but who need some practical ways to get started. Getting started is not as easy as some administrators pretend, but it is not nearly as difficult as many teachers think. In the essays, case studies, practical classroom activities, and bundled software of this book, you'll find what you need to get started.

It may be difficult for you to separate the wheat from the chaff among the available software products, especially when so much of it is so bad, and so much of what is popular is pedagogically shallow. From the outset, some persistent, if unspoken, computer stereotypes need to be set straight.

◆ Computers are not drill and practice machines.

◆ They do not serve much purpose if they are used just for "enrichment" or fluff.

◆ They do not represent a new subject to teach, but rather a new tool to *teach existing subjects.*

Software

Hardware and software each provide their problems for teachers, but the two components are different,with different solutions to their problems.

Part II of this book describes a wide variety of classroom activities that use software with certain desired characteristics, including:

(1) that it fits easily and directly into curriculum priorities for most teachers to teach, rather than representing some new and different subject matter,

(2) that it lends itself easily to use in small groups, as well as occasional "whole class" lessons,

(3) that it motivates students, encourages active learning, and promotes higher-order thinking skills,

(4) that it is easy to get started on, for both children and teachers,

(5) that it is flexible and versatile, so that it can be used in different ways,

(6) that it is readily available to teachers around the country,

(7) that it does not require lots of expensive equipment to use, and

(8) that the same software, or a reasonable "facsimile," is available for the computers commonly available in schools.

One key criterion for selecting each classroom computer integration activity in Part II of this book is how easy the software in it will be for you to use. Look for software that is easy to get started on. For example, if you have never used a word processor, do not start with *WordPerfect*, start with *Bank Street Writer*, a word processor designed for teachers and students. When you want an integrated product–something that combines a word processor, spreadsheet, and database programs–do not start with *Microsoft Works*, a product designed for business. Start with *MindPlay Works*, a product designed explicitly for schools.

Another good idea is to find a piece of software that one of your students is already familiar with, such as *Where in the World is Carmen Sandiego?*. Starting with *Carmen*, you can have the students who have already learned how to use it teach other students, or you. This strategy helps you learn how to use more software and helps your students feel good about what they already know.

Hardware

It is difficult to talk about hardware because your school has what it has, and you must make do with whatever is available. But if there is a choice, many teachers have found that it is easier to begin on a Macintosh than on other computers. Each piece of hardware has some advantages over the other, and this book includes many ideas for using Apple II's or MS-DOS machines, but it is generally accepted that the Macintosh is the easiest for most people to get used to quickly, and with the least emotional stress (for example, feeling stupid).

A useful strategy is to ask your school if you can to borrow a computer to take home. For years, people have been encouraging schools to let teachers take computers home on weekends and vacations, in order to become familiar with the machines. You can take the classroom software along with the computer and become comfortable with it before you have to use it with your students.

The One-Computer Classroom

- **When is one enough?**
- **It take one to "no" one.**
- **What is one to do?**

Jim Smith, a new first grade teacher in a small suburban school, was dismayed to discover that he had only one computer for his entire class, and an old Apple IIe at that. Last year, he had "student-taught" in a school where every classroom had four computers, two of which were brand-new Macintoshes. "What good will one computer do me?" he thought. "I learned how to integrate three or four of them in lots of classroom activities, but what can I do with just one?"

Jim's situation represents one kind of one-computer classroom problem, because he enters the teaching profession feeling confident that he knows how to integrate three or four computers in a classroom. He must use his experience in the multi-computer classroom to figure out how to integrate one computer into his teaching. What is he to do, with just one? You, on the other hand, may be faced with the other one-computer classroom problem: going from none to one. Both of these problems are important because it is most realistic that you will only have one computer in your classroom for the foreseeable future.

How can this be? Presently there are an average of two computers for every 25-30 students in our schools. Since the average class size in America is somewhere in the mid 20's, you might think that most teachers would not have to deal with a situation where they have only one computer for an entire class. Many classroom teachers are lucky to have even one computer available for classroom use, and often that one computer has to be shared with others.

Reasons for this situation vary. Computers are unevenly distributed: between secondary and elementary schools, between affluent areas and poor areas, and so forth. Additionally, within many schools, computers are often locked in media centers, computer laboratories, computer rooms, and the like, so the number available for truly integrated use within the regular classroom shrinks even further.

Therefore, for a long time you will need to know how to take the most advantage of the single computer in your classroom. Luckily, many individual teachers have demonstrated that even a single computer, in the hands of a typical, but competent, teacher can be put to significant advantage in advancing common classroom learning goals.

Knowing how to use one computer to serve an entire classroom simultaneously (rather than a few children at a time) is important to the whole idea of computer integration. A book like *Great Teaching in the One Computer Classroom* (Tom Snyder Productions) can help teachers get a lot more mileage out of a single computer, by illustrating the way the projected computer can be used to introduce new topics, stimulate discussion and debate, or launch a lesson that then continues off the computer.

Some Practical Suggestions

What follows are a number of suggestions for taking advantage of a single computer in your classroom.

1. You can use a computer as a more active and versatile blackboard. Using inexpensive and readily-available connecting devices, you can attach an Apple II computer to a classroom TV monitor, and display the computer screen to your entire class at once. You can then make the blackboard come alive with graphic illustrations, have your students do "board work" that the other students in your class can observe, or run software that readily lends itself to "whole-class" activities. The idea of being able to use the computer to help introduce a new topic to the whole class, of sending children "up" to the projected computer as a substitute blackboard in math, or of using the computer as a dynamic presentation tool, is important, because it helps you recognize how versatile a teaching tool even one computer can be, giving you more incentive to learn how to use it. To connect an Apple II to a classroom TV monitor requires an RGB connector available at Radio Shack, and a few connecting wires. Total cost: about $40.00. (A similar device for the Macintosh is available in the $300 range.)

2. You can use a single computer as a back-of-the-room work station to which you can send two, three, or four students while the rest of your class is working on something else. You can set up a Macintosh in the back of the room (the Mac-in-Back), for example, so that some of your students can be doing independent writing tasks (e.g., adding to a story in process) or skill-related tasks (e.g., peer-tutoring on math word problems), while you are engaged in a whole-class lesson with the rest of the class.

3. For a somewhat greater investment, you can project an enlarged computer screen. The "Macboard" provides certain advantages over projections of other computers: the size of type on the screen can be quickly and easily enlarged to ensure that everybody in the class can read it; the Macintosh can be set up to read the words on the screen aloud; sound effects can be added; etc.

4. You can cycle groups of 4-6 students through a computer center in your classroom while the rest of your class does other small-group, cooperative activities. Or you can teach whole-class activities to the rest of your class, while a small group (perhaps including those children who can benefit most from a set of different activities on the computer) works independently at the computer.

5. You can use software designed specifically for the one-computer classroom (e.g., software from Tom Snyder Productions).

6. You can use a single computer as a peer tutoring tool. Having teams of two students to introduce 2-4 other students to a particular piece of software, provides important benefits to all involved.

7. You can send your single computer home with parents for long week-ends or to be used on vacations. One computer can, for example, be circulated among families of underachieving students in your class, with software–appropriate for family enjoyment–to help raise skill levels.

8. Your one-computer classroom can have a computer center as one of a number of learning centers which you create, through which your students regularly cycle. Others centers might include an art center, a writing center, and so forth.

Telecommunications: A Special Case

Telecommunications, where available, can also help you get the most out of a single computer in your classroom. With an inexpensive modem, access to a telephone line, and the appropriate (and not expensive) communications soft-ware, you and your students can communicate with one another, or with experts and researchers who are helping to give a particular exploration authenticity, across small or vast geographic boundaries. Writing by modem to students at a school in Colorado or South Carolina helps build skills in writing as a way to communicate. It accustoms them to writing in a context more mean-ingful for most than traditional school writing assignments from the teacher. Your students can collaborate on projects and reports with students from around the country.

Although the "relatively" inexpensive materials needed for tele-communications may be beyond your practical reach, some examples of the ways that it is already being used may illustrate its potential. The National Geographic Society's *Kids Network* project uses computing and tele-communications for elementary school children to collect and process scien-tific data (e.g., about acid rain) and transmit their findings across the country. Students become part of an exciting scientific investigation that helps develop skills in doing science, calculating results, writing about it, and appreciating its complexities. Students with learning disabilities in Hawaii are paired with "pen pals" in the Midwest in a situation that promotes meaningful writing experience and produces significant achievement gains. Using an on-line subscription service called the World Classroom, students in Rhode

Island accessed and analyzed data from the National Earthquake Center, enabling them to predict the San Francisco earthquake of the late 1980's shortly before it occurred.

Telecommunications can help prepare your students to use real-life data to make real-life decisions about themselves, their environment, and their world. It will also eventually provide access for them to the proposed national information superhighway. Since full-motion video, as well as text, graphics, and sound, will soon move easily into classrooms over networks, the potential of telecommunications, especially in the one-computer classroom, is enormous.

The Multiple-Computer Classroom

- **The guide at the side or the sage on the stage?**
- **Why put off until tomorrow what you can get your students to do for you today?**
- **Is two *too* much?**

The three groups of second graders on the computers are using The Princess and the Pea. The three groups working off the computers are brainstorming letters they are going to write that pretend to be from the princess, describing what life has been like for her for the past few months. Halfway through the time period, the groups switch; and the groups who have been doing prewriting brainstorming off the computers begin drafting their letters on the computers. Meanwhile, the children who have been using the computers have to fill out a questionnaire that gets them to think about the sequence of the plot. The next day, the groups reverse tasks on a similar assignment.

If you have access to two or three computers, you can explore the many ways in which you can cycle groups of 2-5 students through a set of computer activities while other groups (or the rest of your class as a whole) are engaged in a set of related, off-computer activities. Of the many different models for this type of classroom organization, here are just a couple: (1) Two groups do computer activity A; two groups do related activity B; and two other groups do another, related activity C. (2) One group is off and one group on the three computers for the entire period; the next day they reversed roles; etc. etc. The multiple-computer situation helps you reap the benefits of taking the classroom spotlight off yourself as teacher and focus it on your students as active learners.

Most of the ideas useful in the one-computer classroom can be applied in the two-computer, or three-computer classroom. As computers are added, a greater degree of flexibility becomes available.   Since most classrooms today or tomorrow will have just one, two, or three computers, you will need to learn more "off and on strategies," i.e., ways to orchestrate your class where some of your students work together at a computer while others do not.

The Two-Computer Classroom

Two computers can be used well when you set up learning centers in different areas of the classroom. You can make each a center or put them together in a subject-specific center (e.g., the "computer writing center"). Two computers could also be used to deal with the problem of teaching to the "norm," by teaming some higher–achieving children with some lower-achieving ones as peer tutors (with three or four students at each computer while you work with the rest of your class in a whole).

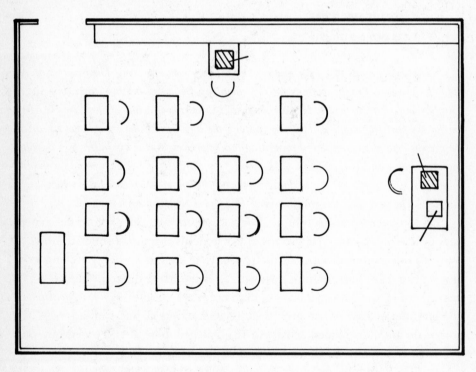

The more software is integrated with the subject matter of the curriculum, the more opportunities exist for cycling groups of students on and off the computer as a part of a lesson that includes some small group activities that require computer use and some that do not. Database activities are a good example, where some of your students can be getting the data they need to enter or analyze (through interviews, encyclopedias, etc.) while others are use the computers for data entry or analysis.

The Three-Computer Classroom

The three computer classroom is probably the minimum needed to make sure that ALL students get some time at the computer during a single classroom lesson or period. Let's say you have twenty-four students in your classroom. If half your class is working in groups of four at the three computers, the other twelve students can be working in three other groups of four on some related non-computer task. Then, halfway through the activity, the on-the-computer groups can switch with the off-the-computer groups.

Three computers can also be effectively utilized in three different learning centers. A first-grade teacher in Tennessee who had six different centers–reading, writing, art, numbers, the city, and science–put a computer in those for writing, art, and science.

Some educators complain that the computer will have no meaning until a computer sits in front of every student. Others counter that such a situation would be the worst thing imaginable. The argument is moot. For the next decade (or more) the reality is that you cannot expect to have more than three computers in your classroom (and you probably cannot hope for even as many as three). Three computers is (as the activities in Part II of this book will clearly demonstrate) more than adequate for you to provide an effective integration of technology into your classroom. If you have one or two computers and some other teacher nearby has two, learn how to plan computer use times jointly on occasion, so that both of you can try things that are possible when more than one computer is available within a single classroom.

Case Study ▬

The Kids Pick *Kid Pix*

This is the story of a newly graduated early childhood teacher, who knew computers could help her students get a real head start. Initially, however, she couldn't convince her colleagues, or her students' parents, that computers were age-appropriate. This case describes how Patty Palomino:

- figured out a strategy for using a single classroom computer;
- helped her colleagues get a feel for the ways computers can complement early childhood learning; and
- "hooked" her children's parents into the fun and excitement of early computer learning.

Patty had just graduated from college in Early Childhood Education, with a minor in Computers in Education. Patty was thrilled to have a job and to be able to use her new skills in a classroom of her own. She couldn't wait to set up the computers for the students. But when she asked her mentor at school about computers, she looked at Patty as if she had suddenly sprouted antlers, and asked, "What on earth would you want computers for? These are little children, dear. They should be running and playing, not sitting in front of machines. Besides, what could young children like these do with a computer? They don't even know the alphabet."

Patty sensed not so much disapproval but discomfort with the whole concept of computers and young children. She knew enough not to rock the boat too much early in her new situation. However, she strongly believed there was a place for computers in early childhood education. She couldn't just forget about it. She decided that one of her goals for the year would be to find an innovative way to incorporate technology into her classroom and the school. Of course, she had one big problem–where was the computer?

Patty knew one of the best allies to have was the school custodian. She had already made friends with him, and enlisted his help in tracking down a computer. After some snooping around, they discovered a Macintosh tucked away in the corner of the school office, still in its original box. Feeling as if she had struck gold, she prepared a written proposal for her principal, who agreed to let her borrow the Mac for three months. The one stipulation was that she would then present an in-service to the other teachers.

Patty wanted the children's first experience with the computer to be easy, fun, and immediately reinforcing. She wanted the children to be able to manage the software independently; and she wanted them to take in stride the whole idea of computers in the classroom. So she introduced *Kid Pix*, a children's paint program, to her preschoolers. For three months, as the children created art with *Kid Pix*, Patty watched their confidence and competence grow. Any observer could see that they truly enjoyed the activities at the Mac. They comfortably accepted the computer as an integral part of their classroom environment. Patty was very pleased.

In her in-service presentation, Patty showed the other teachers what her children had been up to with the *Kid Pix*. Patty explained that the computer was just another activity area in her classroom. She demonstrated the program and let a few of them try it out. They loved the colorful graphics and the wonderful sound effects. Patty pointed out that everyone has a different entry point to new techniques, technology, lessons, or skills.

Patty showed them the portfolios she had created for each child's drawings. Initially, she printed the pictures for the children to keep, but then had also saved their work on a computer disk. Each portfolio contained dated copies of each child's art work, along with notes that Patty had made on their progress. The teachers were surprised and excited about her presentation. Patty was excited about their reaction to her "little experiment."

During her Parent/Teacher conferences, Patty shared each child's portfolio with the parents. Many were interested in how they could encourage their children's exploration of computers. A few who had *Kid Pix* on their home computer requested a disk copy of their child's work. In addition, she obtained the principal's approval to start a week-end loan program, where families without computers could borrow the Mac, along with a book of activities entitled *Parents, Kids and Computers* (Random House), and explore the computer at home with their children.   ▬■

"Most teachers will utilize new technologies only to the degree that they believe that these technologies will help them solve problems that they define as important"

Understanding the
Context

Dear Dr. DeLeet:

I am the mild-mannered principal of a large metropolitan middle
school. I am the very model of a modern instructional leader, but I
have to confess to you that there is no way that I seem able to get my
teachers (who are all wonderful, highly-motivated, and sincere
people) to use all these expensive computers we've bought. Oh,
sure, they occasionally let the kids go play with *Math Blaster* after
they've finished their *real* work, but I sure don't see us getting much
bang for our bucks. I'd like to help them do more,
but I don't know much about computers myself, and,
frankly, I don't want to get the teachers angry at me by
making unreasonable demands. My question is:
What's reasonable?

Clark K, A.B.D.

CHAPTER 3

Barriers to Integration

- **To key or not to key; that is the question.**
- **Is there no fuel like an old fuel?**
- **Out of sight, out of sync?**

When Adelaide Smith heard she could get two computers for her K-1 classroom, as part of a state, "whole school" Chapter I program, she was quick to volunteer. Adelaide always tried to get the latest and greatest equipment for her students.

When her computers arrived at the beginning of the year, she did what she had seen lots of teachers do. She stuck them out in the corridor, and used them to reward children who finished their real work early, by letting them go out and play computer games. Then a funny thing happened. Unbeknownst to Adelaide, the Chapter I people expected her to use the new computers inside her classroom. Even more astonishing, they expected her to integrate them in the regular lessons she taught, and even to make sure that the Chapter I students in her class especially benefited from their use. When Adelaide finally understood these conditions, she quickly withdrew from the project. Didn't these people understand? She had no idea how to integrate these blinking monsters in classroom lessons; nobody had even let her know that that was possible. She had no idea how to organize cooperative learning groups around a computer, and she wasn't all that certain that it was even such a good idea. "Oh, well" she thought, "good riddance to new rubbish."

Why are there so many classroom teachers who still make little or no use of computers in their classrooms? Even *TIME* magazine acknowledges (April 20, 1991) that the impact of technology on the basic operations of most classrooms is "practically nil." What accounts for this inertia?

A Few Theories

One explanation can be based on M.A. Cosden's findings that elementary school teachers overwhelmingly believe that mastery of basic skills is the major benefit of computer use, and that they associate the accomplishment of that goal with drill and practice computer activities. So for the kind of teacher who would be motivated by the other more exciting and more engaging benefits of classroom computer use, the real payoffs are not always apparent. (*Journal of Special Education*, 1988, p. 242-253.)

Another theory, espoused by Larry Cuban, holds that the introduction of new technologies into classrooms in any broad-based way always comes into direct conflict with "the ways schools are currently structured." Asking teachers to risk what seemingly works by trying to meet expectations that are "out of sync" with their organizational realities goes well beyond what "most ordinary, well-intentioned, people" can do. So despite the heroic efforts of the few, who prove what is possible, expecting similar behavior from the many, who work under over-whelming restraints, is unrealistic. Embedded in school organizations are entrenched beliefs about the nature of knowledge, how students learn, and how teachers should teach. These beliefs reshape new technologies to "fit the contours of the setting" and, in so doing, sap their potency. (*Teachers and Machines*, 1986.)

In a similar but more pointed explanation, Seymour Papert, in *The Children's Machine*, traces the erratic history of computers in schools as an exer-cise in "neutralizing a subversive instrument." In the early 1980's, he main-tains, the few computers in school ended up in the classrooms of teachers who showed the greatest enthusiasm. But as computers proliferated, "the admin-istrators moved in" and put all the computers in one room, so students could come together and study computers for an hour a week. By "inexorable logic," the next step was to introduce a curriculum for the computer.

Thus was the computer defined as a new subject. Instead of "changing the emphasis from impersonal curriculum to excited live exploration" by students, the computer became used for reinforcing "standard hierarchical thinking." What had started as an instrument of change was neutralized by the system and converted into "an instrument of consolidation." Papert calls the development of these "misleadingly named" computer labs "a kind of immune response to a foreign body." The logic of the process was to bring the intrud-ing computer "back into line" with the ways of the school.

More Barriers

The barriers that Cosden, Cuban, and Papert describe are real; other, equally plausible, explanations have also been advanced:

- ◆ Those classroom teachers most likely to introduce significant change aren't aware of the most exciting and interesting pedagogical payoffs.
- ◆ The leading manufacturers of hardware and software have aided and abetted the schools' journey down the primrose path of computer marginality, because that path provides the most immediate opening for their products.

◆ Instructional leaders (for example, principals)are not sufficiently aware of the potential value of a few, well-used classroom computers in meeting their most valued instructional objectives.

◆ Too few instructional leaders are aware of available, systematic mechanisms by which *school-wide* classroom computer use can successfully be introduced.

◆ Models of how to deploy effectively the number of computers practically available per classroom (i.e., two or three), though they exist, are not readily available.

◆ Quality standards for separating the wheat from the chaff of classroom computer usage are not readily available.

◆ Nobody has a clear fix on what computers are for, so they are used for this and that, with no sharp vision of their central purpose.

◆ Until very recently, there was not enough exciting, motivating, easy-to-use software to support effective use of computers at every level in every subject.

◆ Many older teachers were never exposed to computers when they were learning to become teachers.

Even among teachers with significant computer experience, Bank Street College of Education researchers found that the majority of the top barriers of the past remain among the top barriers today. Teachers report not having enough time to prepare computer-based lessons, nor enough time in the schedule to include computer-based instruction. They have problems scheduling enough computer time for various classes. Two administrative barriers (help in supervising computer use and financial support) now also figure centrally for these teachers. Apparently, many teachers, although in comparatively advantaged situations with respect to technology, continue to experience the integration of computers into their schools as a struggle for support. (Hawkins and Sheingold, in Culbertson, et.al., *Microcomputers and Education*, 1986.)

Barriers Away

How, then, can we get around these barriers?

◆ On the one hand, we can work on each barrier individually.

◆ We can find ways to make available successful models of classroom integration of computers to teachers and educational leaders as a whole.

◆ We can include instruction in the use of computers in teacher-training programs.

◆ On the other hand, some of these barriers may dissolve over time, as younger, more computer-literate teachers enter the work-force and more and more communities buy more and more hardware.

In the end, however, before most teachers, or principals, are likely to take the time, energy, and effort required to learn about effective uses of computers within classrooms, they need to know whether it is worth it.   Most teachers will utilize new technologies only to the degree that they believe that these technologies will help them solve problems that *they* define as important. And they must be convinced that it won't take some tremendous expenditure of blood, sweat, and tears to learn how to use them.

Knocking Down the Barriers

- **How can you start spreading the news?**
- **Are you manning barricades that don't exist?**
- **Do as I say, not as I do?**

Veronica Gilbey is a second-grade teacher in Denver. Computers have long been a part of her teaching life. But in the past two years, a new program in her school has radically altered her vision of what computers are for. Before she became a part of the Computer Integration and Cooperation Program, Veronica bought into a lot of the conventional wisdom regarding computer usage: "The computer is a great drill and practice tool for slow learners. It is a good motivating reward for when children finish their work early. Today's kids need to get computer literacy skills as early as possible." Then along came CICP, with its alternative vision: training the second graders as computer tutors of children in the kindergarten class downstairs, putting them in cooperative learning groups around the computer, using computers as a basic tool to teach the core subjects second graders have to learn. Veronica now sees a startling difference in what computers can do for teachers: "I used to think of them as just another audio-visual aid to bring in as an extra, but now I realize that they are valuable tools of my trade that provide an important alternative way to help children learn the basic stuff we have to teach," she says.

The first step in getting rid of barriers is to get a better sense of what those barriers are. You have limited ability to break down some of these barriers, but what you can do first is to conceptualize and envision alternatives. Knocking down your own mental and intellectual barriers is as important as increasing the funding of new hardware and more useful software.

Preaching to the Choir

The existence of a core group of computer users in education may make it harder rather than easier to get the rest of the educational community involved. Many articles, books, classroom teaching suggestions, et. al., assume that EVERYBODY can deal with what only this core group understands.

One way to involve the rest is to provide teachers with computer integration ideas and materials that:

a.   address core curriculum issues that are important to THEM,
b.   are relatively easy to implement with limited resources,
c.   go well beyond drill and practice to use methods that good teachers can respect.

Teaching the Teachers

While we have to figure out easy and successful ways to ease teachers who have not used computers into the use of technology, we do not need to hesitate or shrink back from requiring them to learn these new skills. None of us would

use a car mechanic who was unfamiliar with the new electronics that have been introduced into automobiles in the past decade, and we would certainly expect our dentists to have upgraded their tools to meet the changing hygienic standards in their fields. Parents have at least as much right to expect their children's teachers to keep up with the new tools of their trade that can make a crucial difference in the success of the educational enterprise.

Pre-service education programs have to start prioritizing. We must start making intelligent decisions about what to teach the teachers of the twenty-first century about computer use. Pre-service teacher education programs must show prospective teachers how to actually use computers as a tool of their future trade. The first priority should be teaching teachers how to integrate the computer as a useful teaching tool, and the best way to do that, by far, is by example. Teachers of teachers will need to use computers as tools in their teaching before their students can realistically be expected to go out into the field and integrate computers into their own work.

Computers and the Central Focus

The attitude that computers in the classroom are an "extra" creates a mental barrier on the part of overtaxed teachers, who have "important" things to accomplish. Linking computer use to those important things is key to both the quantity and quality of future classroom computer use.

Teacher training must demonstrate in convincing fashion that computers can help relieve the pressure on classroom teachers rather than add to it. To do so requires tying computers to the important, key tasks of classroom instructors, such as learning to solve math word problems, answering comprehension questions about a paragraph, writing a clear business letter, carrying out scientific inquiry, and so forth.

Changing the Decision Makers

Teachers need to have more say about how computers are used in their schools. Principals need to realize that they cannot cede decision-making power over what goes on with computers in their schools to some system-wide computer guru whose main efforts have helped keep most ordinary classroom teachers isolated from meaningful computer use. Principals must understand not just that in-classroom computers *can* make a big difference in the instructional practices of their classrooms, but that they *should already* be making a difference. Even principals who believe in the importance of their roles as instructional leaders are usually not particularly interested in how computers are used in their schools, because they have not yet made the connection between in-classroom computers and instructional leadership. Helping your principal recognize these needs may require some assertion on your part.

Provide a Clear Vision

In many respects, the biggest problem teachers probably face in overcoming the barriers to using computers in the classroom is a lack of vision. To remove the barriers to effective computer use in the classroom, you, your school, or your school system must have a coherent and forceful vision of how computers can be used. This book presents a vision that involves using computers in your classroom to support the central focus of instruction, using software that supports a variety of learning styles and cooperative learning. It is intended to help you develop your own personal vision as the necessary first step.

Integrating Students with Special Needs

- **Is separate inherently unequal?**
- **How can we provide power to the powerless?**
- **What is so special?**

CompuCID (Computer Classroom Integration Demonstration, pronounced Komp-u-kid) pioneered new ways to use technology as a tool to integrate children with special needs in regular classrooms. The CompuCID project: (1) trained teachers to use computers to integrate children with special needs into regular classrooms; (2) trained teachers in how to use the computer as a part of innovative approaches to learning (e.g., cooperative learning); (3) trained teachers (K-8) in how to use the computer as a classroom tool to pursue major objectives of the regular curriculum; and (4) showed teachers how to implement peer tutoring and cross-age tutoring activities around the computer. A manual on implementing this model has been prepared for dissemination by the Foundation for Technology Access in Richmond, California.

The CompuCID project remains an exception to the way most schools utilize computers with their students with special needs. Most descriptions of the use of computers in schools claim that special educators have learned to make more significant use of computers than their regular education counterparts. They acknowledge that special educators are making a greater effort than most other educators to take advantage of the new educational possibilities created by computers. What they do not acknowledge as readily is that what these schools do with their computers often does not really make much sense.

Problems and Problem Areas

In many school situations, the use of the computer with students with special needs is at best a double-edged sword. It may provide the students with greater access to learning certain subjects, but only at the (totally unnecessary) expense of increasing, rather than decreasing, the likelihood that the student with special needs will learn in a segregated setting. Most special educators need to learn how to use the computer specifically as an *integration* tool. Most regular classroom teachers need to know more about how to collaborate successfully with special needs teachers within the regular classroom.

When schools use computers with students with special needs, they far too often utilize them as one-on-one instruments for rote or drill-and-practice learning. This belies two important realities: (a) that such students can benefit more from computer activities that involve learning cooperatively with co-learners, and (b) that computer activities that go beyond drill-and-practice have a more valuable effect on their learning. The computer is also a very important potential socialization tool for students with certain kinds of disabilities. It can help them communicate more easily, more comfortably, and more clearly; facilitate their independence; and help raise their confidence in social situations.

When special educators use computers with students with special needs, only rarely does their work indicate their understanding of how computers (especially the Macintosh computer) can be used as a scaffold to the regular curriculum from which students with special needs are often excluded. For many students with learning disabilities, just the simple ability to use a word processor for writing tasks can make school a vastly more pleasant and successful experience. The computer can facilitate having students with special needs tutor others; being a tutor can prove an invaluable experience in breaking self-stereotypes, and stereotyping by others.

Finally, special educators rarely take full advantage of the possibilities inherent in parent-assisted-learning with respect to computers, or of the potential contribution of siblings in the learning of students with special needs. Computers are still (erroneously) viewed as such daunting instruments that few educators see how willing and able parents, older siblings, and even younger siblings might be a part of the computer-assisted learning picture.

Realizing the Potential

Luckily, there has also been a great deal of successful practice. Below are listed a number of ideas for successful computer classrooms, ideas suggested by teachers with special needs students:

1. Begin with a fundamental belief in the purpose and goals of mainstreaming, and maintain high expectations for all students.

2. Arrange the classroom so that it lends itself to a variety of instructional strategies (direct instruction, cooperative learning, individualized learning tasks).

3. Create a climate for acceptance of experimentation by students and teacher; regard mistakes as learning opportunities.

4. Write lesson plans which focus on problem solving and the process of learning, in addition to the curriculum content.

5. Solicit administrative understanding of mainstreaming goals and assistance in creating resources to deal with the demands that mainstreaming places on classroom teachers.

6. Involve the parents of regular and special education students.
7. Clearly state goals for student achievement; allow opportunities for every student to succeed.

The Computer and Inequality

- **Do poor schools teach to type, not to think?**
- **Why is it that the more things change, the more they remain unequal?**
- **To each according to his/her (special) needs.**

In an inner-city school in Milwaukee, first graders troop down to the Computer Laboratory, to get the only computer exposure they will get during the day. They line up, each staring at a different "dumb" computer monitor. What is in the computer is controlled "downtown," by a central computer administering a networked basic skills program that records the students' achievement progress as they plod through the skill programs.

In affluent schools, students more often get to use computers for creative exploration and higher-order thinking tasks. Teachers in poorer districts concentrate on drill and practice routines for reading, writing, and arithmetic.

Providing equitable distribution of computer resources is one of our biggest challenges. Concerned that the new technologies are widening the gap between the haves and the have-nots, educational policy-makers find themselves with a brand new set of difficult decisions to make. Major problems center on equitable treatment for low-income students, for girls as well as boys, and for low-achieving as well as academically able students. Ironically, like so many educational technologies and innovations preceding it, the microcomputer raised expectations for greater equity and quality in education. Unfortunately, for most school districts, the issues of quality and equity remain largely unresolved.

Economic Inequities

The imbalance in computer resources for rich and poor students is an obvious and pressing aspect of the equity issue. Students with computers at home start with a considerable advantage, an advantage not available to low-income students. Special funding programs and monetary gifts for computer equipment often compound the problem, since the pressure for the use of computers comes mainly from predominantly middle-class parents, who want the district to help their children master the computer.

Achievement Inequities

Differences in the computer instruction offered to students of varying abilities often parallel those described for low- and middle-income students. In many districts, programming courses are provided for students "good in math" and computer-assisted instruction are offered to "disabled learners." In some cases, the vast middle range of students have no contact at all with computers. The educational assumptions behind such ability-stratified usage patterns and the likely educational outcomes need careful examination if these kinds of inequities are to be eliminated. Even when principals in poor schools try to integrate computers more creatively, their plans often fall prey to the following logic of survival. There is enormous pressure to raise standardized test scores. And, paradoxically, rote computer-based training can increase scores by a few points, even while it deadens critical thinking.

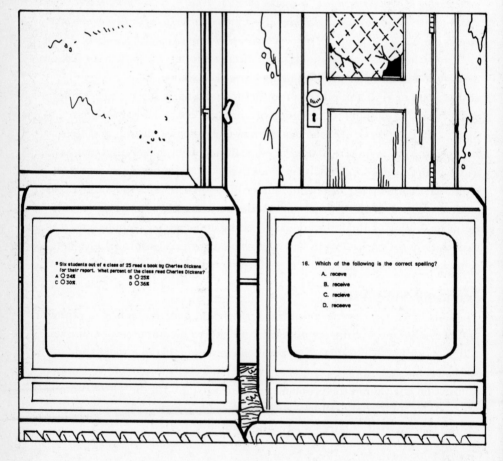

Gender Inequities

Do female students get equal access and exposure to computer opportunities in school settings? Unless teachers are careful, subtle kinds of gender discrimination can emerge. Some observers suggest, for example, that boys gravitate to computers more readily than girls because they are greater risk takers, and thereby "elbow" the girls away from these scarce resources. Others question the kind of gender biases that creep into the software produced by (mostly male) computer programmers.

This book tries to help classroom teachers cope with this issue within the broader context of learning how to exploit the tremendous potential that computers have in helping to accommodate the many differences in learning styles that they confront in any classroom. Basic gender differences and differing acculturation patterns doubtless represent important influences on the learning styles of children well before they reach school age, but schools can reinforce or counteract inequities. Teachers can turn the computer into an important ally in coping with differences.

The Problem Inequities Create

If personal computers fulfill their potential to increase learning, the education gap between learners in the more advantaged strata and those who do not have access to the personal computer will increase. Higher-income learners will become more competent learners and, to the extent that this increases productivity, their income advantage will increase.

One way to deal with computer equity is for local and state officials to press for federal legislation that provides greatly increased funds for poor school systems to train teacher and parents, to make school use more effective and encourage home-borrowing programs. For individual classroom teachers of educationally disadvantaged students, the message is clear: use computers in ways that help students gain control of computers as instruments of higher-order thinking skills, not to prepare them for low-wage jobs operating electronic cash registers or bar codes.

Case Study ■

After School is Cool

This case describes how one early childhood center offered an innovative afterschool program incorporating computers. Karen Davis, director of the center, was surprised by the impact two computers had at her school. Her story tells how she:
- found software which developed basic skills and creativity at the same time;
- motivated her students in a new way;
- generated excitement for learning.

With more and more parents working full time, Karen suspected that an afterschool program would benefit the varying needs of her kindergarten and nursery school children. She sent a notice home to determine how many parents would be interested in this type of program. She was overwhelmed at the response. Many parents were thrilled that the school could provide an alternative to their day care situations.

Karen began to formulate program plans. She was determined that this would not be just a babysitting service. She wanted to make the extended time at school a worthwhile learning experience. From her research, she knew that some extended day programs simply offered "free play." Others included craft activities, nature walks and story-telling. Karen wanted all of these things in her program, but she wanted to include something a little more unique. One idea caught her imagination–the computer. No other program was offering a computer component. Karen knew there was good new software geared to this age. She would need programs which were easy to run for both children and staff and which captured the excitement of learning.

Karen already had one computer, which was being used in the kindergarten room. She was able to acquire another from a parent who was upgrading his home equipment. She set up the computers as additional activity centers from which the children could choose, and decided to gear her program around a set of basic themes that would change every other month. In that way, Karen could structure each center around a theme and the children would have some continuity in the variety of activities available to them for each theme. Karen quickly realized she would need software that was adaptable to more than one theme. She knew "tool" programs –programs which perform a specific function and can be used for variety of purposes–would fit the bill. She investigated software and made her selections from the broad range of available word processing, graphics, painting, and printing programs.

The first month Karen focused everything around helping the kids get to know each other. Using the computer and *Bannermania* (Brøderbund), Karen produced a welcome banner for the first day. It was a bright, eye-catching decoration and the kids noticed right away. They wanted to know how she had done it. She showed them and then created another one with their input and "help." They were excited and wanted to do more.

Using *Kid Works 2* (Davidson), each child, with the help of a staff member, then created a short autobiography which they illustrated with a picture of their family. They printed out two copies and put one up on the bulletin board. The second copy was used to create a class yearbook. Each child took a copy of the yearbook home. The kids loved it. Their parents were delighted with the enthusiasm their children were showing.

In the ensuing months, they focused on the following themes:

- January/February–Teddy Bears. Each child had the opportunity to use *Teddy Bear-rels of Fun* (DLM) to create teddy bear scenes and short stories.
- March/April--Big Books. Using several big book maker programs, *Cute and Cuddly , Letters, Numbers and Shapes, and Favorite Fairy Tales and Nursery Rhymes* (Toucan), children wrote and printed out their own big books.
- May/June--Time. They used a different program during this period. With *Printshop Companion* (Brøderbund), each child was able to develop a calendar of their own birth month, including holidays, etc.

Before they knew it, the school year had drawn to a close. The children, parents, and teachers all were pleased with the learning excitement they had experienced in the afterschool program. Karen was surprised at how much creativity and excitement could take place around a machine. She decided that the computer would have a place in her regular school day, as well.   ▬■

"MAYBE YOU KIDS WOULD LIKE TO
WORK ON THIS PROJECT TOGETHER."

"In addition, frequently the most desirable way to use software that goes beyond drill and practice is in cooperative groups, which can add the documented benefits of cooperative learning to active learning and skill development."

Demystifying the Obvious

Dear Dr. DeLeet:

    I'm in my first year of teaching and, I swear, just getting middle school kids to sit still and listen for ten minutes takes all the energy I can muster. Now my two new Macs have arrived, and the curriculum coordinator has just dropped by with a list of available software and a clear "message" that I am to have the Macs up and running in my classroom throughout the school day. I got some computer literacy skills on the IBMs at college, but they never showed use how to use computers inside classrooms. I don't even know whether any of this software is any good. My questions are: How do I pick the right software (without adding to the stress I'm already feeling)? And then, what do I do with it?

Abandoned in Stressville

CHAPTER 4

Software: the Varieties of Choice

- **How can you keep your eyes on the prize (winners)?**
- **Why AREN'T the best things in life free?**
- **How can simple be powerful?**

Audry had a quick decision to make. Transferred to a new school over the summer, she was delighted to find that her principal had allocated $450 for software for her first-grade class. But she had to decide what to buy within the first two weeks in September, long before she could get to know her new school or her new students. What to do?

How can an ordinary classroom teacher separate the software wheat from the software chaff? Winners of major software awards from publications like *Technology and Learning, Electronic Learning,* and *Media and Methods* help provide some guarantees, but not all of these meet the standards discussed in this book.

There are three major sources of software, each with its advantages and disadvantages. You can buy software directly from publishers, who exhibit at conferences and advertise in magazines. Many publishers offer 30-day trials of their software. Publishers also develop reputations for their entire product line. As a rule, you will probably have luck with software from a publisher with a reputation for quality products, like *Wings, Toucan,* or *Scholastic.*

Most schools buy from dealers or distributors, who sell software from many different publishers and rarely market their own. The main advantage is that you can buy software from many different publishers from one company, using one purchase order. Look for a dealer with a 30-day trial period.

You can buy software from stores, which sometimes even have computers running software, allowing you to try out possible purchases. Many stores, however, do not allow you to return software. And beware salespeople. Many are primarily interested in selling whatever is easiest, and certainly whatever they have in stock. Many salespeople know little about the few educational products they do carry, and they know nothing about the thousands of titles they do not carry. *Caveat Emptor.*

Software Categories

Thinking about software according to categories can be useful–for example, to compare two pieces of simulation software rather than to compare a simulation product with an educational game. Sometimes it makes sense to select a particular piece of software because of the kind it is. What follows is a brief discussion of some of the major categories of educational software.

(1) Drill-and-Practice

This is still one of the most common forms of educational software. It is based primarily on rote learning and repetition. This book avoids D&P software, because it fails to exploit some of the biggest advantages of computers, and is of extremely limited utility.

(2) Tutorials

Educational tutorials tend to be straightforward instructional products. The best tutorials take advantage of some of the special characteristics of the computer: experiments, animations, demonstrations, simulations, rich feedback, and so forth.

(3) Educational Games

Educational games are designed to combine the fun of games with the information needed in an educational product.

(4) Tool-based Learning

In educational settings, software "tools" usually refer to the major productivity tools: word processors, spreadsheets, database programs, and graphing programs. Tool-based learning products use these productivity tools to teach regular content, such as science, language arts, math, and social studies.

(5) Simulations

One of the powers of the computer is its ability to simulate real-life experiences and give students variables over which they exercise control. Educational simulations can be text-only, or include graphics.

(6) Problem-solving Software

Among the first examples of quality educational software was general problem-solving software, which allows students to focus on problem-solving skills as such. Some problem-solving software now also fits specific school content, especially science, math, and social studies.

(7) Educational Adventures

Educational adventures combine some of the features of their consumer counterparts (elaborate game-play, finding lost items, making decisions and living with their consequences, gathering items along the way) with the need to use information (often subject-specific) to answer questions to advance in the adventure.

Software Selection Criteria

One criterion to use in selecting software is cost-effectiveness. Cost, per se, is only a part of this issue. Obviously, if you can get a good word processor appropriate for your students for $50 instead of spending $350, the former is more cost-effective. Generally, the real issue with cost-effectiveness is how many students can use the software how many times. If, for example, you can get all of your seventh-grade science students to use an educational adventure one time each for just an hour, and you have one hundred students each year, even a $100 product is quite cost-effective.

In an age of increasingly scarce resources, flexibility and versatility in a single piece of software become an important software selection criterion. One of the things teachers like about certain kinds of software (such as Tom Snyder Productions' *Timeliner*) is that they can get multiple uses at different skill levels out of certain kinds of software. This is especially true for productivity tools or tool-like programs: word processors, database programs, spreadsheets, etc.

A criterion that is more rarely mentioned is how the software fits the kinds

of instructional strategies the teacher prefers. Because this book favors pedagogical strategies that support inquiry, cooperative learning, problem-solving,
etc., we have chosen software and classroom activities that lend themselves to
such strategies in Part II, which presents practical classroom activities. In selecting software, you look for consistency between the software and your own
instructional strategies of choice.

Finally, many educators talk in terms of a criterion that reflects the power
of the computer: interactiveness. Books cannot be interactive, and computer
software can be. Therefore, look for software that is truly interactive. What
characterizes interaction? Look for software that calls for thoughtful action on
the part of students and that provides feedback when they answer questions
incorrectly. Look for software that offers your students variables they can
control. Look for software which can adjust to different students at different
levels of ability (intellectual or computer skill). These are some of the characteristics of truly interactive software.

A Word About Shareware

Shareware–public domain software–often (although not always) costs very little
money. You may not have to spend more than a few dollars for this software,
unless you like it and/or want the printed documentation, at which point you
have to/can send in a little more money. Some of this software is quite good,
but most of it is, at best, spotty. It is generally not professionally packaged and
often not well tested or debugged, and it usually lacks developer support. Just
keep those things in mind. On the other hand, the software situation is not as
simple as: "You get what you pay for." A lot of commercially-available software
at much higher prices is not much better.

Software Serving Two Masters

- **Can you kill two birds with one mouse?**
- **Round up the unusual suspects.**
- **Check your hidden assumptions at the door.**

In the teen movie Pump Up The Volume, *Christian Slater plays a high school
student who uses his guerrilla radio station to bring down an unscrupulous high school
principal. The principal's crime? Cutting off the school's underachievers from opportunities to stay in school in order to pump up her school's standard achievement test*

results. Her (erroneous) assumption? That only with high-handed, old-fashioned, hard-nosed drill-and-practice methods could her school preserve its reputation as a "winner." Slater wins his battle under the usual preposterous teen movie circumstances. Yet the film manages to make an interesting educational point: Maybe there is a better way to produce achievement in basic skills.

This book takes a similar position regarding the choices that you can make with the software you integrate into your teaching: there is a way to use computers to promote the basic skills still overwhelmingly valued in our schools *without* having to resort to dull, drill-and-practice software.

An important prerequisite, however, is the need to check your stereotypes at the door. A key obstacle to realizing what is now possible with computers is the too-common association between increasing achievement levels and using one-on-one, drill-and-practice, basic skill software. This book takes an alternative view: that avoiding drill and practice, using learner-centered software and methods can lead to significant achievement gains–gains that show up on standardized tests. At the same time, doing so will develop the kinds of learning skills that make *future* achievement gains more likely!

In addition, frequently the most desirable way to use software that goes beyond drill and practice is in cooperative groups, which can add the documented benefits of cooperative learning to active learning *and* skill development.

Basic Skills

The definition of what constitutes basic skills is undergoing rapid change. For example, the new standards of the National Council of Teachers of Mathematics emphasize that students should work with "real-world related" problems in mathematics lessons. A software simulation, for example, can provide students with a motivating format for running a small business, stock an inventory, and determine a selling price for their product. Solving word problems is also a focus of the NCTM standards. Learning to *write* math word problems may do more for the development of problem-solving ability than tackling math word problems alone. Activities that allow students to create a survey and then graph the results, or enable students at the elementary level to develop a sense of geometry can help them to more easily advance to higher mathematics. The mathematical skills necessary for students in the twenty-first century will also emphasize working collaboratively in groups to solve problems, using technology as tools in this process.

Software Alternatives

A number of different kinds of "electronic books" illustrate some of the ways that software can promote active learning and maximize student achievement. Software products like *Just Grandma and Me* and the "Discis Series" are designed to help students develop reading skills and fluency. Such programs can read the story to the students as they highlight the words. Students can click on words to get definitions. Most of these programs have animated illustrations, and many allow students to interact with the book in a variety of ways. Such programs hold promise as alternative ways to "teach" basic reading and code breaking skills.

Even elemental software tools like word processing programs can promote basic skill without resorting to drill-and-practice methods. A number of word processors on the Macintosh, for example, can function as reading as well as writing tools. Many such programs allow students complete freedom to write (active learning) and then can read what is on the screen back to the student.

A Concrete Example

More and more, school-based projects are being explicitly designed to insure that the software they involve will serve these two masters. The Teacher-Led Computer (TLC) Project in Arlington, Massachusetts set out to do precisely that. Classroom teachers use software that teaches reading comprehension, solving math word problems, writing about science, and following scientific method, among other skills. TLC trains classroom teachers to integrate computers into their day-to-day classroom work, in a way that has a direct impact on the improvement of students' achievement scores, without recourse to drill-and-practice software.

The project's goals focus on

(1) promoting achievement gains,

(2) enhancing students' ability to think for themselves, and

(3) helping teachers learn how to combine cooperative learning techniques with computer technology.

Such practices suggest that basic skills enhancement is not just a legitimate goal, but a very desirable goal, *when linked* to exciting instructional methods and appropriate ways of evaluating accomplishment of the achievement goals. Assume a software tool exists that will help you teach the content in the way you want to teach it. Then develop the software finding skills to "round up the unusual suspects." Finally integrate learner-centered software with skill-building classroom activities.

Multi-Media Alternatives

- **Do you have to walk the walk before you talk the talk?**
- **The future isn't what it used to be.**
- **The more the merrier?**

(1) In a suburban school outside of Detroit, pre-kindergarten teachers spend the first 20 minutes every Monday, Wednesday, and Friday introducing beginning science concepts through the "magic" of interactive videodisc. Then the machines are shut off, classes go back to the "status quo ante media," and no other teachers in the school get to touch the new multi-media equipment.

(2) A team of second-grade students sits at a computer connected to a videodisc player and completes a series of "interactive" lessons, keyboarding answers as the program progresses. While the students are focused on the solution of a dastardly environmental crime, they are learning important information about the eco-structure of the shore, to solve a mystery closely related to the ecology curriculum mandated for their grade. When they finish, they start a non-computer activity involving analysis of the school's drinking

water, while a new team uses the interactive video equipment to participate in an adventure involving math word problems.

These two stories illustrate the pitfalls and potential of multi-media materials. When multi-media materials are used outside the boundaries of the regular classroom curriculum, their use is severely limited and may not justify their expense. On the other hand, when they are thoroughly integrated into the core curriculum of a regular classroom, they can offer exciting ways to engage the attention and various intelligences of a wide variety of students.

What is Multi-Media

So, what exactly is "multi-media," this wave of the future that already exists, in a fashion? As with so many new phenomena, there is no precise definition. Put most simply, multi-media products combine video, audio, textual, and graphic material. These materials typically require a hardware configuration that combines a computer with a videotape player, an audiotape player, a CD-ROM player, and/or a video/laser disk player.

Multi-media products have two distinct advantages over computer software products. First, multi-media products usually allow for the storage of vast quantities of information (both text and visuals). CD-ROM platters and videodiscs hold immense amounts of information compared even to typical computer hard drives, let alone floppy disks. Thus, these products can put vast amounts of information at teachers' and students' fingertips.

Second, multi-media products tend to be highly visual, because multi-media hardware can store so much information, including high resolution color photographs and video. Thus, multi-media products look and feel much more like television than like typical computer software.

What are the Problems?

Until very recently, one big problem with multi-media was analogous to the problem educational software as a whole had during much of the 1980's: the lack of high quality material to fit the existing curriculum. As a result, most people using it used it for extras and enrichment, rather than in a truly integrative fashion. Although this situation will change over time, keep in mind that lack of quality material still defines most educational software. As a multi-media problem, it will continue even longer.

A second key problem with implementing multi-media materials is its costs and perceived benefits. Costs for equipment and multi-media materials are still relatively high. Having a computer simply is not enough; you must add a CD-ROM drive, a VCR, or a videodisc player. And multi-media software can cost from 2-3 to even 4-5 times the cost of computer software (although costs are falling). Until people perceive benefits to justify this cost, multi-media will be at a disadvantage compared to computer software.

And the Advantages?

One advantage of multi-media activities is their ability to help make the abstract concrete. For example, in *Jasper Woodbury*, students watch Jasper and his friends encounter real-life problems that must be solved by using math skills. Research shows positive effects on problem-posing, problem-solving, and student attitudes towards math. Students can deal with important math topics like decimals, fractions, geometry, measurement, estimation, and statistics within exciting, highly-visual, real-world situations.

Multi-media also can fill in some missing needs for visual learners, who are often at a disadvantage the way schools usually teach. Multi-media makes possible actually showing your students things that you could previously only talk about. Multi-media has the potential to help schools meet new mandates to relate classroom activity to the variety of intelligences that every student brings learning situations, and to adjust to the growing number of students who do not thrive on the highly linguistic, logical-mathematical learning model that dominates most classrooms.

A big future advantage of multi-media is teacher empowerment. Multimedia can let you pick and choose, from among a much wider variety of options, what information you want to present your students.   A parallel advantage for students may be the non-linear feeling of control and ownership it may give them. The potential of multi-media is tremendous, but the practical realities inhibiting that potential (small amount of product, unusually high development cost, high acquisition costs, limited perceived value) are, for the moment, even greater. It will justify the cost only AFTER multi-media products exist that:

(1) fit easily and snugly into the regular curriculum that teachers are under the gun to teach,

(2) clearly support student achievement gains, for teachers who are under pressure to promote them,

(3) support the kinds of active learning styles that innovative teachers (who are the ones more likely to buy into technology in the first place) seek,

(4) help classrooms adjust to the needs of mainstreamed students with learning disabilities and differences, and

(5) offer teachers sufficient flexibility and multiple uses to justify the extra cost of the materials.

Computer Hardware

- **If you've seen one, have you really seen 'em all?**
- **Why do you gotta play the hand that's dealt?**
- **All computers are equal, but are some more equal than others?**

Jill Hardy was the new kid on the block, but she was ready to attack his first teaching assignment with all the new knowledge at his command. Her college professors had prepared her for the classroom of tomorrow; she knew how to deal with interactive video,

CD-Rom, MTV, VCR, RCA, Hypercard, and even Hyperventilation. But wait, one lousy Apple IIE? This was not what she expected.

The fundamental hardware question used to be: What computer do we buy? That is clearly an important question still, particularly for administrators and computer coordinators charged with purchasing hardware for their school systems. But the development of educational software has now reached a point where the fundamental hardware question for you is: How do I get the most out of what is available?

Today there are hundreds of thousands of computers in American schools. Whereas in the early 1980s, there were more brands than anyone wished, the current trends are:

(1) The Macintosh has replaced the Apple IIE and the IIGS as the Apple computer of choice for school systems.

(2) Secondary schools get new IBMs (or clones) and Macs.

(3) The elementary schools still have more old Apples than anything else.

As a result, you cannot use the excuse that you have got the wrong computer anymore. Some computers may be better than others, but there is some good software available for all these machines, and it is worth learning how to get the most out of the one that you happen to have access to.

If You Can Buy

Although this book is a practical guide for teachers who do not usually get a chance to choose their computer hardware, teachers are sometimes able to influence new computer acquisitions. When buying new machines, school systems need to start making hardware choices with a greater eye towards ease of use for the technological neophyte.

The most obvious example is the Apple Macintosh, the "computer for the rest of us" that, for most users, is easier to begin on and easier to use than either the Apple II or the IBM. The Macintosh also has specific advantages for children with disabilities. Used with the right utilities (e.g. ACTA), spell-checkers (e.g., MacWrite II, which catches phonetic misspellings), etc., it can make writing activities far more pleasant and reinforcing for a large group of children formerly alienated from this task. Especially for the older, experienced teachers who have not yet integrated computers in their classroom teaching (i.e., most of the classroom teachers in the country), ease of initial use can have a profound effect on reinforcing or diffusing unspoken stereotypes about whether technology is worth bothering with.

Hardware Makes Hardware Easy

In the early days of educational computing, teachers had so many kinds of computers available for purchase that they hardly knew where to begin: Apple II+, Apple IIe, Apple IIc, IBM-PC, IBM-PC AT, Tandy, TI 99/4A, TRS-80, Commodore 64, Commodore 128, Atari, Sinclair, MSX, and on and on. Now the choices are MS-DOS and Mac.

Another factor inhibiting the integration of computers in classrooms is the noise from a dot matrix printer. For some teachers, the noise these printers generate seems overly intrusive and disruptive of the kind of learning environments they want. The advent of the relatively inexpensive laser, or ink jet, printer can eliminate this concern.

Software Makes Hardware Easy

Interestingly enough, one way to make computers less threatening relates to the software that accompanies them. We have to stop thinking that programs like AppleWorks and the Apple IIGS are easy just because an in-group of 10-15% of the teachers have put in the time and effort needed to master them. To encourage teachers to take risks with computers in their classrooms, it is critical to purchase software that is genuinely easy-to-learn and easy-to-use. Many students may have little trouble learning AppleWorks, but it is surprisingly difficult for many teachers. An example of a less well-known, but noticeably easier-to-learn, piece of software is *MindPlay Works*. It was designed for the same purpose as the more well-known integrated packages, but it was designed specifically with teachers and students in mind.

Case Study ■

Hard Software Choices

This is the story of a director of an early childhood program who was determined to propel her center into the twenty-first century by introducing the many facets of technology to her school. The case describes how, after extensive research, she:

- decided to forgo the comprehensive (and expensive) bundled software packages available to her;
- discovered that individual software programs provided her with a more cost-effective and flexible approach to technology than the comprehensive bundled software packages; and
- chose software that focused at the same time on BOTH teaching basic skills and higher order learning skills.

Eighteen months ago, Jill Mindess, director of the Ridgefarm Preschool, attended a workshop at the New England Kindergarten Conference. The workshop awakened her to the many ways in which computers could enhance an early childhood program. As she rode home from the conference, she vowed that she would bring her school into the modern world of technology.

Her first step was to get funding. She learned from various articles that money was available through various grant resources, and obtained a list of current grants from her state Department of Education. She quickly applied for a grant which seemed appropriate for her needs. To her great surprise and delight, several months later, her school received a mini-grant in technology. She was off and running.

But running where? She needed to catch her breath and do a careful assessment of how best to spend this limited amount of money. She first had to prioritize her hardware and software needs and for that she required assistance. Through the local university, Jill found that there was a very active computer using educator (CUE) group in her area. She called them and discovered that they sponsored a conference every fall, which as luck would have it, was just three weeks away. Jill immediately signed up to attend with two of the teachers on her staff.

At the conference, Jill acquired a great deal of information. She learned that choosing hardware was directly tied to decisions about software. Conference exhibits enabled her to preview many of the available software programs. She was particularly impressed with programs which taught basic skills with a creative, problem solving approach. These were the higher order thinking skills she wanted to encourage. The "drill and practice" method of learning would not meet her goals.

There were several very comprehensive (and quite costly) products that were clearly outstanding. Examples included:

- *Tapestry* (Jostens)–a comprehensive integrated early childhood curriculum covering early math and reading readiness. The program includes software, books and tapes.
- *Stories and More* (Eduquest)–a program designed to promote child centered learning as it reads the stories.
- *Early Language Connections*–a comprehensive learning program which incorporates reading, writing, listening and speaking. This package includes the hardware as well as the software solutions.

Jill also saw wonderful programs published by companies such as Sunburst/WINGS for learning, Great Wave Software, William K. Bradford, MindPlay, Davidson, Edmark and a host of others.

After the conference, Jill and her fellow teachers spent time reviewing journals and resource literature on early childhood software. Two of the best publications they came across were *High/Scope Survey of Early Childhood Software* (The High/Scope Press) and *Only the Best:Annual Guide to Highest-Rated Education Software/Multimedia for Preschool-Grade 12* (Education News Service). Jill knew that she had enough information to make educated decisions on how to best use her grant money.

She really liked some of the bundled software packages and understood they had some distinct advantages. But when she considered all of the factors, she decided that they would not be the best alternative for her teaching needs or budget. Instead, she chose a selection of software programs which included *Kid Pix* (Brøderbund), *Kid Works 2* (Davidson), *Millie's Math House* and *Baily's Book House* (Edmark), *Playroom* (Brøderbund), *I Love You in the Sky, Butterfly* (Hartley), *McGee* (Lawrence), and *Print Shop* (Brøderbund). Her mini-grant, had helped her to start moving her school into the twenty-first century.   ■

QUALITY TIME

"Teachers around the country have discovered a useful little secret: they can get parents to help them do their job--by sending classroom computers home with learner-centered software over weekends and vacations, by providing the growing number of families who now own computers with loaned software and at-home learning activities, etc."

Exploiting the Computer's Full Value

Dear Dr. DeLeet:

    I teach in a large, inner-city school, in a *very* heterogeneous class-room. Many (most?) of my students seem to have some kind of learning disability or reading disability, but I never had any special training in these areas. What I do have are these three new Macintosh computers, which are better than the one I have at home, and a special program budget to buy a reasonable amount of soft-ware or "peripherals." This may be a one-time opportunity, and I don't want to blow it. My problem is: I don't feel I know enough to make the kinds of decisions I have to make in the next few months. My question is: What's the quickest way to find out what I need to know?

                                    Teaching for America

CHAPTER 5

Cooperative Learning

- **Is cooperative learning and computers a marriage made in heaven?**
- **Why doesn't competition compute?**
- **Can computers cooperate?**

Darrell, a student in an inner-city school in Charlotte, North Carolina, is reporting to his second-grade class on the progress his group of five students has made on its computer assignment. "Number One: How carefully did we check? We checked very carefully. Number Two: Did we help each other? We did very good on that. Number Three: Did we encourage each other? Err... that is where we should do a little better next time. Number Four: How well did we teach each other? We did that very good."

One of the biggest misconceptions of the computer is that it is designed for individual use. Clearly, individual use of the computer is important in theory. It is the most important use of the computer in business. But learning as an individual exercise is not always, or even most often, the most appropriate or effective pedagogical strategy.

Benefits of Cooperative Learning

Cooperative learning has become a central pedagogy in many classrooms, for its instructional, social, and emotional benefits. The computer can often be more effective within a cooperative learning environment than within an individual-oriented one. Cooperative learning humanizes the computer by enabling you to incorporate children with widely divergent learning styles and abilities within the same group, especially when used with the right software. That is why this book emphasizes using the computer as an element of cooperative learning.

Research suggests that achievement and problem-solving skills can be increased when students work together around a computer. In one such study, for example, the effects of computer-assisted cooperative, competitive, and individualistic instruction were compared according to skills achievement, student-student interaction, and attitudes. Computer-assisted cooperative learning (1) promoted greater daily achievement, (2) led to more successful problem solving, (3) produced more task-related student-student interaction, and (4) increased the perceived status of female students. (Johnson, *et.al.*, "Comparison...," *American Education Research Journal*, Fall, 1986.)

What is Cooperative Learning?

Cooperative learning is a way of structuring student-student interaction so that:

◆ students know they can be successful only if their group is successful,
◆ students are accountable for their individual understanding and mastery of whatever is being taught,
◆ students receive specific instruction in the social skills necessary for the group to succeed,
◆ students have the opportunity to discuss how well their group is working and receive feedback to improve future performance.

Learning in groups on a computer is not synonymous with cooperative learning. Turn-taking that occurs when students share a limited resource like a computer involves a degree of cooperation, and students agree to abide by the rules of sharing, but the learning activity may still focus on the individual.

In cooperative learning, you set up varied opportunities for your students to explore "curricular content" along with other learners. These opportunities make your students co-active manipulators, rather than inactive recipients, of information, concepts, and problems. The key to cooperative learning is interdependence. The members of the group must need one another and have a stake in each other's understanding and success. Cooperative learning reinforces your role as "guide on the side," while the use of carefully selected software assures you of the quality of the content available to your students.

Structuring Cooperative Learning

Much software may be used as easily with small groups as with single individuals. Students can solve problems independently, compare answers, discuss disagreements, explain their respective approaches and solutions, and reach agreement on what to enter into the computer. To structure a cooperative computer activity:

(1) Assign your students to groups of two or more with at least one member who is able to run the computer program and one who is task-oriented. A teacher who takes cooperative learning seriously does not arbitrarily create groups; the composition of cooperative leaning groups is as important as their existence.

(2) Instruct students to alternate roles, such as keyboarder (enters data

once there is agreement within the group), explainer (explains how to work the problem or the rule needed to respond appropriately), and group reporter (Darrell's role in the scenario that began this section).

(3) Provide needed materials. Do not throw students in groups and leave them on their own; as much teacher preparation is needed for cooperative learning groups as for whole-class activities.

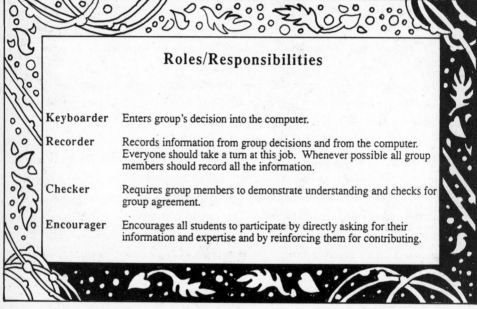

Roles/Responsibilities

Keyboarder Enters group's decision into the computer.

Recorder Records information from group decisions and from the computer. Everyone should take a turn at this job. Whenever possible all group members should record all the information.

Checker Requires group members to demonstrate understanding and checks for group agreement.

Encourager Encourages all students to participate by directly asking for their information and expertise and by reinforcing them for contributing.

(4) Assign the task of completing a specified number of problems. Students in cooperative learning situations should have as clear and explicit expectations as in any other learning situation.

(5) As a criteria for success structure positive interdependence by requiring students to reach agreement on their responses before entering them into the computer.

(6) Once students have begun, monitor how effectively the groups are working together and fulfilling their role assignments. Students in cooperative learning groups need as much teacher attention as in any other classroom organization.

(7) Ask groups, at the end of the lesson, to discuss briefly how well they worked together and to decide on a behavior they could adopt next time to promote each other's learning. Cooperative learning groups

put students in positions of power and responsibility, and taking as active a part in the evaluation of their own learning as they do in the learning process itself is important.

Advantages for the Teacher

Teachers who have used traditional learning groups find that requiring individual accountability insures that each student contributes to the group. It helps you monitor exactly how much each student has contributed and mastered the target skills. In a cooperative computer activity, for example, each student must be able to explain the activity, produce a printout, or score at a certain level on a quiz. All students must know in advance that they will be responsible individually for demonstrating mastery.

Computers for Accommodating Diversity

- **Why not let a hundred computers bloom?**
- **How is diversity the mother of invention?**
- **Can we think of thinking as a basic skill?**

A computer consultant has been brought in to help "revitalize" a state's thinking about computer use. She began: "I am glad you could all make it to our in-service series. I did not realize there were so many North Carolina teachers interested in using computers as a tool for accommodating the diverse learning styles, levels of learning, and special learning needs of different individuals." Then she offers two examples:

1. First grade teachers in Tennessee used cooperative learning-by-doing activities around a computer to integrate recently mainstreamed "underachievers" in their classrooms, using math software that simulates math manipulatives.

2. A fifth-grade teacher in Colorado paired students who were her greatest underachievers with her brightest students, and trained them as cross-age computer-tutoring teams, to work with small groups of first graders, thus giving the tutors greater self-esteem as well as a way to "learn by teaching."

She then asks her audience to take a few minutes to think of two more ideas for using the computer to accommodate diversity. [When you've finished this section, think of a couple yourself.]

American classrooms have probably never done a great job of accommodating the diversity of learning styles and abilities in their midst, and now classrooms are getting more diverse just as pressures are growing for raising academic achievement, focusing more on higher order thinking skills, and reducing pullouts of educationally disadvantaged and special needs students. What is a teacher to do?

One clear problem is that contemporary American education too rarely acknowledges, fosters, and takes advantage of the diversity which it increasingly encounters. Some educators even blame their failures on diversity, instead of looking to diversity as a way to increase their success. The computer can provide students with learning disabilities, physical handicaps, or simply previous school failure with fresh entry points for learning and communicating, opportunities never before experienced in schools.

Letting Computers Bloom

An initial approach to using computers to accommodate diversity was to marry Benjamin Bloom's taxonomy of thinking skills with software for computers. Bloom's six thinking skills are:

> (1) knowledge,
> (2) comprehension,
> (3) application,
> (4) analysis,
> (5) synthesis, and
> (6) evaluation.

Each skill is important, but education in many classrooms often ignores "higher-order" skills of analysis, synthesis, and evaluation. To apply technology to remedy this deficiency, some software developers created programs that addressed the development of higher-order thinking. While many drill-based programs reinforce development of lower-order skills, the catalogs of a few publishers (e.g., *Wings* for Learning) are filled with programs to help students learn how to analyze complex situations, create solutions from a synthesis of existing parts, and articulate the thinking processes leading to a solution. But such software is only the beginning of the possibilities.

Multiple Intelligences

Computers provide for a rich variety of teaching strategies, accommodating to widely divergent learning styles and special learning needs.   Within a single classroom, they enable you to address all seven intelligences that Howard Gardner has identified in *Frames of Mind*: Linguistic, Logical-Mathematical, Intrapersonal, Spatial, Musical, Bodily-Kinesthetic, and Interpersonal.

Gardner believes that, while each of us may dominate in one of these seven areas, we all have capabilities in the other six. The atmosphere in today's classroom often reinforces the tendency to teach to the linguistic, logical-mathematical, and intrapersonal learner, and virtually to ignore the other four intelligences. Our tendency to teach exclusively to the linguistic, logical-mathematical, and intrapersonal learner has two negative consequences. First, it ignores the needs of the child whose dominant intelligence is not one of these three. Second, it misses the chance to validate and develop the other intelligences in all the children in the room. Time and again we have found that, the more ways a subject is presented, the better the subject is learned and remembered. Gardner's work illuminates a new path for education, one that can do much to help children retain their natural love for learning.

Multiple Intelligences and Computers

How can a teacher use the classroom computer as a tool to meet the needs of a variety of students? How is the teacher to tailor a curriculum to different intelligences? Since the start of the computer revolution, we have been told that this technology would allow the individualization of instruction. Now with Gardner's powerful theory to guide us, we can bring that dream into sharper focus. We can explore the match between the software we have and the dominant intelligence of each child. We can highlight areas for which new software needs to be created and develop specific sets of criteria by which such software can be judged. This focus has been missing in educational computing.

The Rabbit is the Enemy?

- Is the whole equal to the sum of a bunch of little parts?
- Are teacher-proof computers also learning-proof?
- If the shoe fits, don't wear it?

Miriam, a first-grade teacher who went through school in the 1950's is painfully aware of the criticisms that upper-grade teachers are always making of the system's students: Kids do not have the faintest idea of what makes a paragraph, or even how to string two simple sentences together; they are not prepared for intermediate math; they cannot spell; they think grammar is Grandpa's wife. Partly as a result, Miriam runs a teacher-led classroom where children put in lots of time learning the basics they have not picked up yet. She lets the high achievers do extras, enrichment activities, etc., but the noses of the rest of the children she keeps to the basic skills grindstone. Miriam's questions are: Can a computer help them learn vocabulary? do math problems? write a clear sentence?

Teachers just starting to use computers inside a classroom, whether veterans like Miriam or beginning teachers, are like customers in a shoe store—they are looking for a comfortable fit. Something that fits their image of what is important to do in a classroom, what is important to learn in that classroom, and how to organize the class to learn it. But they do not know much about all the software choices available to them. It is not "one-size-fits-all" or a "customer is always right" situation. Instead, it's a situation where the universe of choice is limited, with an overwhelming number of choices being made in favor of drill and practice software. Is this good? Bad? Irrelevant?

Why Is a Bunny an Enemy?

In his book, *Insult to Intelligence: The Bureaucratic Invasion of Our Classrooms* (1986), Frank Smith calls *Reader Rabbit*, a best-selling, step-by-step, drill-and-practice package "the enemy." For Smith, the rabbit (and much of the other software used in classrooms) is a symbol of a programmatic approach to instruction that simple-mindedly pretends that children learn by practicing one disjointed systematic piece of learning after another. Children, he contends, cannot learn anything "one fragmented, trivialized, and decontextualized bit at a time." The educational computer industry, he believes, has developed in a way that confines children's learning in precisely this way, and is supported by administrators, professors, special educators and other experts who do not trust teachers to teach whole subjects to whole children.

Those who want to use the computer as an "intelligent" electronic tutor or stand-alone drillmaster are not necessarily doing something harmless. If Smith is right, much of the software on the market is either intentionally or inadvertently designed to support backward and even repressive pedagogy, which can get in the way of efforts to help students see language as a whole, become "fluent" in math, or experience the practical value and uses of communication.

You need to know what to reject, and why, as well as what to look for. Be careful not to use software that reinforces the tendency (already present in too many schools) to chop content into little unrelated parts, in an effort to spoon-feed it to students who teachers think have difficulty swallowing it whole. Rather, you should look for software expressly designed to reinforce whole language methods, to encourage question-asking as well as question-answering in math, to help your students discover the value of scientific method, to understand how a historian gathers evidence to back up conclusions, etc.

Can Drill Not Kill?

Other people claim that there is room for drill and practice. They point to programs like DLM's *Math Facts*, which works to develop speed and automaticity, or Intellimation's *Software Drill for the Mac*, which some excellent teachers have claimed to use quite creatively. Proponents of this kind of software argue that it is not the software's fault that learning is "fragmented, trivialized, and decontextualized."

Even proponents of drill and practice software usually agree, however, that such software is not the optimal use of technology in learning. Their perspective is that drill and practice software is useful IF it is used "where it belongs" in the learning process. They say that a teacher always needs first to get students receptive to what they will be taught. Next, the teacher should tell students what is going to be taught and provide them with information and mechanisms with which to manipulate the information the teacher presents. Finally, the teacher should provide the students with guided practice, with teacher support and intervention as necessary.

If all of these steps have been followed, they argue, then the "rabbit" may legitimately enter. After students have mastered the material, the teacher can turn them loose to do drill and practice on their own, in order to get better and faster. Where many teachers falter, they say, is when they jump immediately to the drill and practice, without the "teaching." *Reader Rabbit*, like all the other stand-alone software equivalents, does not teach anything. It just provides practice on material presumably mastered. Like any product, proponents of drill software argue, it does not work if it's misused.

Down with Drill

That response misses the point. The software industry is perpetuating and reinforcing an already existing and unfortunate trend in American education. When software breaks up learning into disconnected pieces, it is all that much harder for you to come up with "methods and strategies" that pull the pieces back together into a meaningful whole. If, for example, you are teaching a "whole language" approach, of what value is software that divides the whole into apparently unrelated and unconnected parts? If your students need to get "better and faster" at a particular skill, we already have lots of materials that do not tie up the computers. As TIME Magazine has suggested, flash cards are a lot cheaper. Computers are too valuable a resource to squander. Use them for what they're good at, to promote powerful pedagogies.

Promoting Parental Involvement

- **Aren't some teachers parents?**
- **Aren't some parents teachers, too?**
- **Are parents the first teachers? the worst teachers?**

The scene: an elementary school in one of the most culturally diverse neighborhoods of El Cerrito, California (and probably of the country). A drawing is being held at a pre-Christmas parent assembly, to see which families will get to borrow the school's Macintosh computers over the Christmas vacation. As the winners are announced, a first-grade girl begins jumping up and down–she cannot contain her excitement at her family's good fortune.

Scenes like the one above are all too rare in America's schools. Yet those who are interested in raising achievement levels in our nation's increasingly diverse school systems would do well to note the rich benefits such activity provides: increased parent involvement (which correlates closely with increased student achievement); creative use of computer "down time" (most of the computers in our schools are turned off for many more hours than they are on); greater trust between school and community (a growing need especially where the student population is culturally different from the teaching population); and increased volunteer time from parents (some of whom then spend volunteer time within the school as well as at home with their own children).

Parents as Resources

Teachers around the country have discovered a useful little secret: they can get parents to help them do their job–by sending classroom computers home with learner-centered software over weekends and vacations, by providing the growing number of families who now own computers with loaned software and at-home learning activities, etc. Their thinking is rooted in some solid research, which suggests that increased parental involvement in a child's schooling leads directly to increased achievement. By learning how to help parents use the computers sensibly at home, these classroom teachers reap the achievement benefits of increased parental involvement with very little extra effort and very little extra cost to the school.

These teachers are tapping into the incredible potential of at-home computer activities as an adjunct to schoolwork. In contrast to traditional home work assignments, these "home fun" activities can more comfortably and more readily incorporate participation by parents and/or siblings, while still yielding big returns in student achievement. And this is only the proverbial tip of the iceberg. Imagine what teachers could do by regularly inviting parents to ally with them in doing things in the home that not only increase parental involvement, but also offer parents "quality" recreational time with their children, enhance sibling cooperation, and improve parent attitudes toward the school.

Examples of Parental Involvement

A number of school systems are already showing the way:

◆ In Charlotte, North Carolina, a fourth-grade teacher recruited a small group of parents to come to an after-school class to learn how to use computers with children, then induced them to volunteer to help her support small-group activities around her three computer stations.

◆ In Commerce City, Colorado, two paraprofessional aides (themselves parents of children in the school) organized and conducted an evening computer class for parents, as part of a weekend and vacation computer lending program. The system's computer coordinator reported some interesting results of this activity: Parents who took computers home said they were "very pleased that the school would allow this to happen." The loaning of equipment fostered a "feeling of trust and cooperation between the school and home" that had not been present before.

◆ In Arlington, Massachusetts, a group of parents volunteered to learn how to train other parents as classroom computer aides, enabling teachers to get help, for example, in supporting several cooperative groups working simultaneously on different subjects and problems at different learning stations.

◆ In Indianapolis, Indiana, fourth graders in pilot schools got "buddy" computers to keep at home during the year. Parents became more involved; students wrote work of higher quality and greater length and complexity; and students made gains in self-esteem.

Techniques to Involve Parents

All these programs rather cleverly take advantage of growing parent interest in computers, the growing willingness of parents to participate more actively in their child's learning, and the eagerness of a small but significant percentage of parents to get involved in, and give time to, their children's school. Other techniques include:

1. Giving parents who already own computers "consumer advice" about software that is fun yet still supports what the teacher is trying to do in class. A school in Massachusetts, for example, offers parents (and grandparents) reprints of software reviews just before Christmas, and guidance about where the software can be obtained at the cheapest prices.

2. Helping parents to acquire computers, either by giving them good consumer advice about how to get the best deals on the best computers, or even, in some cases, establishing systems by which parents can borrow funds to purchase computers or participate in a computer loan fund.

3. Establishing software loan programs, enabling parents to try programs before they buy them.

4. Organizing PTA or PTO sales of inexpensive learning software, as an alternative to the candy sales of the past.

5. Offering computer training to parents, for career advancement as well as student support purposes.

6. Providing circulating computer lending programs (like the one in El Cerrito) during weekends and school vacations.

Teachers are also using computers to change the way they communicate with parents. Here is how one experienced teacher described an aspect of her teaching most teachers do not even think much about:

> It was easy. I wrote a form letter and just filled in different names. I had to write the letter only once; the computer printed it out over and over. I customized each letter with specific comments about each student's performance.

One teacher has researched the effectiveness of this kind of letter writing. Parents responding to the survey were overwhelmingly in favor of the letters they received. Most parents perceived the form letters as written specifically for them. The survey results also showed that parents felt that they received more information from the teachers when the teachers used the computers than they did when more traditional methods of communication were used.

Case Study ▬

Early Cooperation

Lori Vaughn, an experienced kindergarten teacher, always had children in her class who couldn't seem to understand cooperative learning. In this case, Lori discovers how, with only a single computer, she can:
- successfully teach cooperative learning and sharing concepts;
- effectively accommodate diverse learning styles ; and
- encourage and integrate cooperative learning in all aspects of her classroom.

As a kindergarten teacher, Lori Vaughn believed that sharing was one of the most valuable skills she could teach her students. She knew it was a skill they would use in every facet of their lives. She also knew it was one of the most difficult lessons to learn. In spite of her efforts, there were always children in her class who had particular difficulty working with their peers. Over the years, she had accumulated and used many different activities which focused directly on sharing and cooperative learning. No matter what she did, some children were unable to grasp the idea of sharing, even in a play situation.

Last year, Lori was surprised and pleased to have a new addition to her classroom: a computer. She had read that the computer could enhance and enliven her teaching, but she hadn't heard that it might be helpful in promoting cooperation. From the moment the computer arrived, however, she discovered that one computer would force her to create cooperative situations.

The children were immediately interested and intrigued with the computer. But they quickly realized that if they wanted a turn, they would have to work in pairs or small groups. Lori began to research software that would fit this style of learning. She got excited by one book in particular. It was called *Great Teaching in the One Computer Classroom* (Tom Snyder Productions). The premise of the book was that one single computer can provide a rich variety of teaching strategies and activities in the classroom. Based on many of the points the book made, Lori researched and chose software for her kindergartners.

As the year progressed, Lori experimented with different types and styles of software. She focused on those which promoted cooperation and cooperative learning.   Not all of her choices were winners. She found that not all programs worked with all types of children.   Sometimes what looked great in the catalog totally bombed when she used it. Lori became quite an expert on preschool software. She found that some programs accommodated diverse learning styles better than others. Some worked well for everyone.

One program, *McGee* (Brøderbund), was a hands-down winner for all of the children at the beginning of the year. It is a non-reading exploratory adventure about a little boy in his home. The majority of Lori's students soon moved on to more complex programs. Some of her special learners, however, found reassurance in the simplicity of the program's routine and stayed with it for a good part of the year. They were happy at first just to watch as the other children used the more difficult programs. But they were learning that way and eventually, they too moved on.

Lori discovered several other programs that were fun and effective in developing cooperative learning skills.

- *Reading Magic Library Series* (Tom Snyder Productions)–a group of simple stories where students decide what happens next to branch the story to a conclusion.
- *The Living Book Series* (Brøderbund)–a series of interactive programs on CD based on popular children's storybooks.

Lori carefully selected the pairs and small groups of students who worked at the computer with these programs. With her guidance, the children learned to alternate roles as keyboarder and encourager or explainer. It was especially rewarding to see her special learners being guided by peers. She began to see how peer teaching fostered social development. One day, Lori watched as one of the most reticent children confidently explained to the others, how to add things to the screen in the *Explore-a-Story* program: *Princess and the Pea* (William K. Bradford).

In other aspects, as well, cooperative learning had became an integral part of life in Lori's classroom. What the children had learned at the computer was unconsciously carried over to other activities. It seemed so easy. Lori had discovered the natural synergy between the computer and cooperative learning. ■

PART II

Part II of this book is comprised exclusively of practical classroom activities. Each activity is designed to enable you to put it to immediate use. We utilize five different and distinct formats in presenting these activities:

Lesson Plan

This format includes a series of categories (teacher preparation, materials needed, procedures, follow-up, and so forth) which structure the information. The Lesson Plan is the category which includes step-by-step instructions or procedures.

Unit Plan

The Unit Plan format is designed to describe a series of activities that take place over time, often a week or more. Each Unit Plan divides its materials into a small number of categories, categories which vary from unit plan to unit plan.

Up Front

In the Up Front format, the teacher doing the activity describes that activity. All the information you need to implement the activity is still included, but in a different, more personal style, with a focus on the reasons why a teacher has done certain things.

From the Sidelines

In From the Sidelines, an observer in the classroom describes what is happening. Each account concludes with a Teacher's Response, where the teacher doing the activity can respond to what the observer has written.

Kids' Perspective

The Kids' Perspective format allows students doing the activity to describe what happened, sometimes in their own words, sometimes through their work.

The classroom activities are not clustered separately into these five categories. We have purposely mixed up the activities to create some variety in what you are reading and to make it more enjoyable for you to "shop" through the various kinds of activities available.

Lesson Plan

BIRTHDAY TIME LINES

Purpose
This lesson will help students use utility software to understand how their own birthday is related to other birthdays. As students think about birthdays over the course of a year, they receive practice in sequencing.

Materials
Timeliner, Tom Snyder Productions (Apple & IBM version)
Mac Timeliner (Macintosh version)

Preparation
The software allows children to make a timeline about their birthdays. Become familiar with the version you choose before introducing it to students. *Timeliner* can be used by the youngest of children, with a little adult support. (The Apple version is quite simple. The Macintosh and IBM require a little more help.) You may wish to display around the room graphic reminders of the children's birthdays (balloons, a train of cars, an octopus, etc.).

Precomputer Activity
Have the children gather around, and start with a question: "What is something that we all have?" Elicit a lot of answers–the children will probably say things like eyes, hair, teeth, etc. Move the topic toward birthdays by asking, "But how about a special day, just for us?" When you get the right response, go on with a discussion about birthdays:

- What is a birthday?
- What does our birthday celebrate?
- Why is each of our birthdays different?
- How do you celebrate your birthday?

[NOTE: If some of the children are adopted, keep in mind that they may not have been told about their biological parents.]

You may wish to read a story to the children about birthdays, possibly about how children of another culture celebrate on their special day. If you have children in your room from another culture, ask them to bring in anything special that is used for a celebration at home. Then explain to the children that they are going to make a timeline so that everyone will know when their birthday is, and where it is in relation to all the other birthdays in the room. Be sure to explain what a timeline is: a chart that shows in order when things take place. This is an excellent opportunity to integrate practice in learning the months of the year, days of the week, etc.

Computer Activity

❶ Show the children the program *Timeliner,* and explain that they will be keying in only two things:

(1) the month and day of their birthday (example: September 18)

(2) their full name (example: Susan Ami Wentworth)

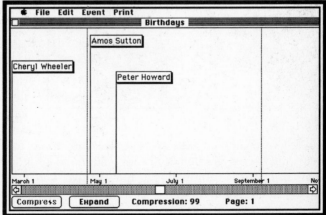

❷ One of the wonderful features about *Timeliner* is that, unlike the old paper and pencil timelines that teachers struggled with in years past, this timeline will automatically readjust itself each time a new date is inserted. Therefore, the order in which the children go up to the computer does not matter; the timeline will come out in the right order every time.

❸ Put up a wall chart with the children's names grouped in pairs. Then have partners go to the computer and enter their data. (If you feel that you need an adult volunteer or an older child to help, have the helper at the computer only for assistance as needed.)

❹ When the children have all entered their information (enter your birthday also), the timeline is ready to be printed out. (The children love watching the printing process; however, if you feel the printing time is too long, print out the timeline after hours.) It might be advisable to use the *Expand* feature on the program to elongate the timeline just a bit for the follow-up below.

Follow-Up

Find a back wall or a bulletin board in the room where you can stretch out the timeline. Then, over the next few school days, have each child go up to the timeline, find his or her name entry, and above it draw a small self-portrait. You are left with a wonderful product that can stay up in the room all year long.

Up Front

A MOVING ANIMAL EXPERIENCE

Children have a special fascination with the other creatures with whom we share the earth. Perhaps this is why one of my favorite units in my kindergarten focuses on animals. And our newly acquired classroom computer adds a whole new dimension to our study of animals! I have discovered a wonderful early childhood program: *Learn About Animals*. This program is informational and creative, and the children become completely immersed in it.

There are sections on:

- Animals and their Homes
- Animals and the Foods they Eat
- Animals and their Babies
- Animals and How they Move
- Animals and their Size, and
- The Worlds of Animals, plus
- A Creative Section on making your own funny animals, and
- A Mask-Making Section

One of the many great things about this software is that it's largely self-correcting. A child trying to match up an animal to its home, for example, moves the squirrel to a knothole in the tree. If the response is correct, the squirrel automatically climbs in when placed close to the right spot. If the response is incorrect, the squirrel will just sit there. If the children are matching up an adult animal to its babies, the babies will "nestle" in with their parents.

I spend several days on each section of the program, playing related games, exploring the software, and reading related stories. To illustrate how I integrate different activities, I'll describe how we work with the section, "Animals and How they Move."

To stimulate some discussion, I tell the children that we will play a pantomime game. We sit in a large circle. I get in the middle, and move like a certain animal. The children's job is to guess which animal I am. After I do one pantomime, the child who "guesses" my animal gets into the circle and does another one. Then, we talk about slow animals and fast animals. I follow this by playing different paced music as the children walk around the room imitating an animal at a corresponding pace. We stop, and share who our animals were.

My next step is to establish several activity centers for a few days, based on "Animals and How they Move." Let me describe the centers.

1. Magazine Center - I put out lots of magazines containing pictures of all kinds of animals. (The National Wildlife Federation's magazines are great for this.) Each child gets a sheet that looks like this:

FAST   SLOW

The children's task is to cut out pictures and place them in the right category.

2. Computer Center - *Learn About Animals* is in the computer already booted up. I have the children go from the Main Menu to the MOVE section. They see a screen with the directions "Put each animal above the word that tells how it moves." With an assigned partner, the children follow these instructions to match an animal with its way of moving. As in the other parts of the program, this is self-correcting (a boon for teachers!). If the answer is correct, the animal stays above the label and moves in place; if incorrect, the animal keeps moving across the screen.

The children work with other sections of the program in a similar way, and I provide accompanying activities that relate to the topic. After the children have worked with all of the informational sections, we have a special culminating activity. I have the children, again working in pairs, go to the Create section of this program to make their own funny animals. The program allows them to combine heads, bodies, and legs of their choice. Then, with the help of a parent volunteer, I have the children write a short story about their animals. We use *Muppet Slate,* and most of the children dictate as the parent writes. I like to encourage a few of my beginning readers and writers to try to work on their own. The children use a story skeleton that is on a file and is ready for them to fill in. It looks like this:

MY FUNNY ANIMAL

This is _____ (name: They can incorporate their own name or make up a silly one.)

It lives _____.

It likes to eat _____.

It has _____ babies.

It moves _____ (slow, fast).

I especially like it when my animal _____.

With the help of my parent volunteer, the children print out their animals and their stories, and we have a wonderfully imaginative bulletin board, fully created by the students.

Teacher Tips:

Software

Learn About Animals, Sunburst/WINGS for learning (Apple, Macintosh)

Lesson Plan

KID PIX RIDDLES

Purpose
To help students (PreK-1) associate a picture with its vocabulary word, and to familiarize students with riddles.

Materials
. (Apple, Macintosh, IBM)
Stamps and stamp pads, paper.

Preparation
This lesson assumes that the teacher has done some previous work with the children in introducing the program *Kid Pix*. *Kid Pix* is a very versatile graphic-based program with a myriad of potential uses, both in the classroom as well as at home. Users can create from very simple to very complex pictures using the many different levels of menus available. For very young children, there are several options available. One is what they call the "Small Kids Mode." Another wonderful feature of *Kid Pix* for young children is the Stamp Section, which is what this lesson employs.

Precomputer Activity
Provide lots of opportunities for children to create pictures using stamps. Stamps are available in so many varieties - alphabets, numbers, holidays, animals, etc. You can adapt several art activities to whatever else you are doing in class, but the purpose would be to foreshadow your on-line work at the computer with stamping in a concrete way.

Computer Activity
❶ Gather the children (whole class or small group) in front of the computer, and review for them how to move within *Kid Pix*, and particularly how to get to the "Stamps" area. Next, go through the stamps slowly, so that you are sure that they can identify all of the pictures. The stamps are quite small on the screen, so you might choose to (a) either do this in small groups, or (b) stamp them onto the drawing screen larger (this can be done using various keystrokes). If you do this, show the students how to do it as well; it is quite easy.

❷ Talk to the students about what riddles are. What *are* riddles? Questions, with answers. Tell the students that they are going to try to solve some riddles using the stamp pictures for the answers.

❸ Next, try some riddles together. For example, type in using the text mode: "Starts with a D, and is a toy." Have one child come up to the computer and look through the stamps until they find an answer: DOLL. Let them try stamping that next to your riddle. Try a few more:

Starts with an S, shines outside.....　　Answer: SUN.
Starts with an M, shines at night....　　Answer: MOON.
Starts with a T, drives on the road...　　Answer: TRUCK.

❹ After several youngsters have tried, pair the children up and tell them that their job is going to be to make up 3 riddles (you can do less with younger children). Have them look at the pictures in the stamp section, pick three they like and make up the riddle with the answer. For preschoolers or pre-readers, you could have an adult help with the keyboarding. For early readers, let them try typing in the riddle themselves. Have each pair put three riddles into the computer, skipping at least five lines between each one to make room for the picture answer. Save each one with the children's names.

❺ At this point, the riddles can be shown in several ways.
　a. Each file can be retrieved, and together with the group, you can try to solve them.
　b. Print out all the riddles. Then print out large copies of each of the stamps needed to solve a riddle. Reprint your riddles on large tagboard strips, and laminate both the strips and the stamp pictures. Put them on a bulletin board and let the students try to match their homemade riddles with the picture answers by tacking them together. Kids will play with this over and over again.

Follow-Up

The *Kid Pix* stamps can be integrated in many other activities. Here are a few ideas:
　(1)　Picture dictionary - have the children create a letter dictionary, giving them help typing in the word next to the picture. Have them use the same letter of their name, if you like.
　(2)　Set up a *category* activity. Create an activity set of pages that say things like:

FIND ALL THE THINGS IN THE SKY
FIND ALL THE THINGS THAT MOVE
FIND ALL THE ANIMALS

97

From The Sidelines

CLIFFORD, THE BIG RED DOG

This was my day to help out at my daughter's preschool class. Every parent had been asked to volunteer at the school at least once every three weeks. Although many parents grumbled about this, I really enjoyed it.

Amy and I arrived at the school a little early so I could help her teacher, Mrs. Goldberg, set up for the day. Joan Goldberg informed us that the children were celebrating Clifford that week. *Clifford, The Big Red Dog*, by Norman Bridwell, is one of Amy's favorite books. Amy proudly showed me a large Clifford stuffed dog that she explained was visiting their room for the week. She told me that he normally lives in the office with Mrs. Paraboshi, the Director of the school. As I looked around at the many activity areas, Joan pointed out a special activity for "Clifford" week. The children would be making their own droopy ears, like Clifford's, to wear. Joan had set out on the table a number of cardboard "ear" patterns. The children would be tracing them onto red paper (because Clifford is red) and then cutting them out. The children would then attach the ears to a strip of paper that would fit over their heads. Besides being fun, this would help refine their fine motor skills in tracing and cutting.

Joan then explained that she wanted me to assist the children in creating their own storybooks, with the help of the computer. She and Amy guided me over to the computer corner. Amy showed me the computer and the monitor, which she said "shows things in color." She pointed out the printer, where "our words can come out on paper." Joan explained that we would be using a program entitled *Clifford's Big Book Publisher* (Scholastic), and she had Amy show me how to insert the disk into the disk drive of the Apple II computer. After Amy turned the computer on for me, Joan suggested that I try out the program with Amy's help. She could be the first student to make her own book.

The first screen we saw showed Clifford holding the "Main Menu." I used the arrow keys to highlight "Make a Big Book" and then pressed <Return.> I then chose "Start a New Page" on the next screen. The "Page Menu" listed all of the tools we would need to make a book. First I chose "Decorate," which gave me the three options: Background Graphic, Clip Art, and Frame. In the back of the manual, I found pictures of the 31 background graphics available.

They were wonderful.

Amy chose the one that showed Clifford reading a book. This was fun and easy. By following the simple step-by-step directions in the manual, Amy and I were able to create a big book. Amy dictated a wonderful tale about Clifford reading a book about Morris the Moose (Amy's other favorite storybook character.) I was really amazed at the appearance of the finished copy when we printed it out. Amy chose to make her book in the "Big" size, so it printed out 17 by 22 inches. She loved watching her creation come out of the printer. With her help I carefully pieced the four sheets of paper together to form each page of her book.

When Amy finished, Ryan was patiently waiting to create his big book. This was to be a terrific morning for the children and me. By the end of the day, I was not just "Mr. Harris," I was also "Amy's Dad who helps us make our own books."

As Amy and I drove home, she chattering about the birthday party they were going to have for Clifford, I thought about how technology is changing our children's schools. These children were growing up feeling comfortable with computers. Amy's generation would not be made up of computerphobics - like mine. Amy, who at 3 1/2 could not read or write, already considered herself an author. Her Big Book, proudly on display in the class reading corner, was proof. Learning was indeed fun.

Teacher Response: _____

The Clifford Software is available from Scholastic.

Up Front

SNOOPY WRITER

As a pre-school teacher, I often encounter disbelief when I tell parents and other pre-school teachers that I believe it is important to introduce writing at the nursery school level. Young children love to tell storie–the more outlandish the better. Why not capitalize on this? This doesn't mean that the children are pushed to form letters before they are ready. But with our Apple II computer, and a wonderful human helper, my children have become authors.

Our class is located in a nursing home, and the residents have become a regular part of our classroom scene. One gentleman volunteered to work with the children on the computer, provided I showed him how. He told me that he had witnessed his grandchildren using that "new fangled thing" and he thought he should give it a try. I decided that this would be a perfect opportunity to encourage my children to become published authors.

I explained to Mr. Martin that I hoped he would help the children write their own books. The children would dictate a story to him and he would act as their scribe. I told him that I had a software program called *Snoopy Writer* (Random House) that would make this very easy. I showed him how get the program going in the computer. The menu appeared on the screen broken into four sections, each depicted by a picture showing an activity. I suggested that we compose something for the children. He chose "Write" and immediately was presented with three options: To Begin Story, Create a Picture or Begin Writing, or Go Back. Mr. Martin chose Create a Picture and was given the choice of four settings - Beach, Camp, Stage, or Party. He chose Party (because he loves to boogie). He then had a choice of characters: Franklin, Pig Pen, Schroeder, Frieda, Charlie Brown, Lucy, Linus and Sally.

Once he had decided on all of these details, it was time to write. Together we penned a little story about Charlie Brown becoming a famous author. When we finished, I showed him how to print out his story. Talk about being proud! I also showed him how to save the story to disk and how to use the story starters that are available, in case one of the children got stuck for an idea.

When I arrived at school the next morning, Mr. Martin was waiting. I reminded him that the stories were to be the children's creations. He assured me he understood. I explained to the children that Mr. Martin was going to help them write their own books. We talked about what should be in their books - a cover with a picture on it and a story that others would want to read or hear.

Michael reminded us that the books should have their name on it . I then let Mr. Martin explain to the children that he would be working with them one at a time and that everyone would have a turn during the coming week. He asked the children to be patient with him as he was new at using the computer. They assured him that they would help him. Since it was Joelle's birthday, all of the children agreed that she would be the first to write a book.

Joelle and Mr. Martin went off to the computer area and quickly became engrossed. As I had suspected the children were not at a loss for words. The stories poured out of them. At one point I heard Mr. Martin promise Billy that he could write another book as soon as everyone had a chance. Once their stories were printed out, Ms. Patti, my assistant, guided the children in adding illustrations, making a cover, and binding the books with yarn or ribbon. (Some of the children were tired of sitting still, so their stories were put on a special shelf for them to finish later.) The completed books were carefully placed in the new authors corner I had decorated. This area, adjacent to our book corner, has comfortable pillows for the children to sit on while they carefully "read" one another's books.

Book writing and publishing became an on-going activity. Mr. Martin was joined by other residents of the nursing home in helping the children, but he remained the expert. As the school year progressed, I introduced other word processing programs such as *Once Upon a Time* (Compu-Teach), *Muppet Slate* (Sunburst/WINGS for learning), and *Cotton Tales* (Mindplay). The children became more proficient writers as did our older helpers.

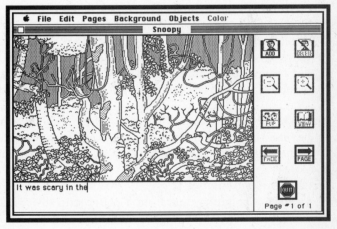

Mr. Martin became so entranced with the computer, he began to input stories he had heard as a child. I helped him graduate to a more complex word processing program that he used after school. In return, he promised to share the results with the children. His stories were priceless. My children gained so much from their interaction with these warm, loving people. And they developed a love of reading and writing that I am convinced will be with them throughout their lives.

Teacher Tips:

Once Upon a Time (Compu-Teach), and *Cotton Tales* (Mindplay) are also available for the MS-DOS platform.

Lesson Plan

NUMBERS ON THE LINE

Purpose

This activity is designed to provide students (K-1) with visual representations and experiences to develop understanding of basic addition and subtraction facts. Students work with number lines in a concrete way to develop understanding of equations in both addition and subtraction. Students develop strengths in basic addition and subtraction facts by manipulation of concrete objects on a number line, and learn to write a variety of equations for one problem.

Materials

Paper Tape, assorted small objects such as plastic bears, rods, small baskets or boxes for groups to collect their objects, overhead projection device for demonstration of program. Recording device for working with program. Software: *Hop to It* (Sunburst/WINGS for learning)

Preparation

Teacher should review the program and explore teachers manual to understand the sequence of difficulty at each level. Students should be grouped by fours to complete the activities. Roles are materials manager, recorder, encourager/timer and keyboarder. These activities are flexible and each member of the group could rotate roles for additional experience. (Strengths of students with special needs are emphasized by working with cooperative groups. Specific roles of these students within the groups should be based on particular learning styles and strengths. These students in particular should be encouraged to verbalize their observations and strategies.)

Precomputer Activities

1. Make a counting tape from a paper strip to facilitate counting/addition activities which can be attached to the floor/wall for hands on student use.

2. Develop experience with the words associated with movement on the paper strip (number line) such as jump forward, jump backward as well as counting the steps.

3. Place small objects or toys on the paper number line for collecting. Have students explore the variety of ways in which to collect the objects.

Computer Activities

❶ Using an overhead projection device or large screen monitor demonstrate how the program works. Use student volunteers as soon as possible in the demonstration to work the keyboard. Encourage students to look for multiple solutions for collecting the objects on the line. Ask questions such as: How else might Bonnie have collected her vegetables?

❷ Students continue to work with the program in small cooperative groups. Use Recording Sheet for further concept development and evaluation.

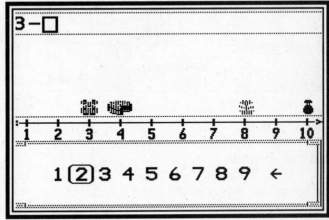

❸ After each group has had sufficient time to work through the first level of the program, have a large group discussion of discoveries made by students working with the software.

Follow-Up

- Utilizing the seven levels of this software continue to allow students to progress through the activities.
- Using rods make a variety of rod trains and write equations for the train.
- Provide opportunities for students to write and draw stories utilizing the characters from the software program.

Up Front

TEDDY BEARS FOR TEA

One of the best ways to involve young children is to use some of their own possessions, and among the most treasured of these is a child's "teddy bear." A wonderful theme for a creative writing adventure is "teddy bears," with each child's own bear as the star performer. With the help of your classroom computer, and the software *Teddy Bear-rels of Fun,* you can provide such an adventure.

In his landmark book "Mindstorms," Seymour Papert discusses computers in education. Papert points out that children learn best when they begin with experiences closest to their lives. By using a theme children can relate to, along with a desktop publishing program, you can encourage both oral and written expression.

Begin by asking the children to bring in their teddy bears for a week. This could present a problem if the teddy bear is also a "lovie," and one that cannot be omitted from the nighttime routine. In that case, ask the parents if (1) an alternative bear can be sent in, or, (2) if the parent can be responsible for making sure the bear comes into school each morning for a week. The latter can be a difficult task, so the former would definitely be the better choice. A third alternative, which might work best, would be for you, the teacher, to have a cache of extra bears available for anyone who forgets. Also have a "class bear" available.

Once the bears are in school, tell the children that they are going to pretend that the bears have come to school to have a tea party. If you have a pretend play center, you can actually set this up; if not, improvise. At the tea party, the bears are going to tell the class about some exciting trips that they have taken. Let different children speak for their bears and tell where the bears have gone.

This activity is particularly good for students with deficits in oral expression. For all children, it will get at crucial aspects of the core early language program in an exciting and motivating way.

The next step is to show the children the program *Teddy Bear-rels of Fun.* In this desktop publishing program, the children can create scenes of many different types, using teddy bears as the main characters. There are beach scenes, seasonal scenes, windy day scenes, etc.

Using your class bear, ask the children to pick a scene where they think the bear might have traveled with his/her friends. Once the scene is picked, follow through the program to create that scene. In the program, the user is given the choice of:

(1) Background scene: to create the theme.
(2) Types of teddy bears - big, little, pairs, etc.
(3) Props for the scene.
(4) Balloons for anything the bears might be saying.

When you have completed the scene, go to the word processor component of the program and show the children how you can create a short story about your scene.

When the children begin to create scenes, have them work individually or in small groups, depending on their age. Once the scenes have been created, have the children go to the word processor and dictate or write a short story explaining their bears's exciting trip. The amount of keyboarding your students can do will depend on age, reading ability, and skill with the computer. However, parent volunteers as well as older children can be of great help here.

These stories can then be printed out and made into a class book for all to share. You might even want to have your children sponsor a tea party for their bears, where cookies and "tea" are served and the children read their stories to the bears.

Teacher Tips:

1. If you are doing a whole unit based on teddy bears, there are many offshoots to this activity, both on and off the computer.

2. There are numerous storybooks about bears in the library (*Winnie the Pooh*, the *Little Bear* books) for you to put out for the children to explore.

3. You can use *Teddy Bear-rels of Fun* to create bear stationery, signs, posters, comic books, greeting cards, and bulletin boards.

4. You can create teddy bear pen pals in the older primary grades, with the children's bears writing notes to each other.

5. There are other computer programs based on bears. Some are listed below. Use these primary programs and others to create an exciting variety of stimuli about the world of bears, both real and imaginary.

Software:

Teddy Bear-rels of Fun, Apple, IBM

Teddy & Iggy, (Apple, IBM)

Balancing Bear, (Apple, IBM)

Teddy Bear's Picnic, (Apple)

Berenstain Bears (IBM)

Lesson Plan

COUNTING CRITTERS

Purpose

This lesson offers a math component to science lessons on animals, for grades Preschool through Grade 1. It reinforces important readiness skills: number recognition, counting, making comparisons. It also introduce the concept of sets. Practice is provided in a context children can relate to through their own concepts, rather than through rote drill.

Materials

Flannel board; flannel shapes (six different animals with a varying number of each); flannel numbers, cut out (with number dots on the back to make them self-correcting); container for flannel shapes and numerals (Apple II computer(with 64K), color monitor (optional), one disk drive; *Counting Critters* (MECC).

Preparation

This lesson naturally follows a science lesson on animals. Have materials ready and be familiar with the software program.

Precomputer Activity

Encourage the children to discuss what they have learned about wild animals: elephants, giraffes, tigers, etc. Ask them to name some animals, and place the matching flannel animal down the right side of the flannel board. Then have them help you count the number of different animals on the board. Be sure to point to each animal. Explain that each group of animals can be called a set. A group of things that are alike are a set. Next, have a child help you place the flannel numbers in numerical order, with each number opposite an animal going down the left hand side of the flannel board.

Extend this activity by removing all of the flannel figures and placing the numbers across the top of the flannel board. (Have a child assist you.) Have another child put a different kind of animal under each number. Help the children observe that you have many elephants, tigers, lions, etc. in the cage. Have the children take turns picking an animal and placing it under the matching animal. When all the animals have been freed from their cage, ask the children if the number of animals under the number one matches the number one. Continue this for number two, and so on.

Follow this with questions such as:

How many different groups of animals are on the flannel board?

How many different numbers do we have?

What kind of animal makes up a set of 6? of 3? (etc.)
Which set has more in it, the set of tigers or the set of elephants?
Which set has the most? Which set has the least?

Computer Activity

❶ This activity may be done during Circle Time, or it may be set up in the computer area with an adult or older child assisting the children.

❷ Have a child insert the disk in the disk drive and turn on the computer. When the main menu appears, select COUNTING SAFARI. This program will reinforce counting skills as well as the ability to identify the numeral that corresponds to a matching set. The screen will show Charlie Chimp swinging from the tree. Around his tree will be a number of matching animals. The children must help Charlie count the number of matching animals that he sees. The children then match the number of animals they count with one of four numbers in a list. When they answer correctly on their first try, Charlie will jump up and down, clap, run to the end of the branch, or swing from the branch.

❸ There are three chances to answer correctly. The first incorrect answer prompts the animals to flash one at a time (encouraging the children to count them). A note on an ascending scale is played as each animal is flashed. A second incorrect answer prompts the program to number the animals. If the children miss a third time, the numbers show up below each animal and all choices except the right one then disappear. Once the children have answered ten, they will see a screen that shows their score in a pictorial and numerical fashion. The children answer each problem using the hand-shaped pointer that appears. They just move the hand to the answer they select and then press the RETURN key. Those children who are more familiar with the keyboard can enter their answer by pressing the number keys. Have the children take turns helping Charlie. Encourage them to verbalize what they are doing.

Follow-Up

Two additional components to this software program can be used to reinforce future lessons. PET STORE and COUNTING POND follow the animal theme and offer the children more opportunities to practice their skills. Each component may be used in a large group setting during Circle Time, in smaller groups during activity time, or by individual children.

Notes

This portion of the program is set to the numbers 1 through 10. Teachers may modify this to include 11 and 12. Access the Management Options at the Main Menu. Hold down the Control Key and the letter A. Sound is also an option that can be turned on or off at the Main Menu.

Up Front

MOST IMPORTANT LETTERS

Am I crazy? Everyone in my school is scrambling around, looking over their shoulders, afraid that someone will see that they are not having a child touch the computer that day. It's become an obsession – if you don't have the kids on computer tasks, you better watch for that pink slip. Well, my feeling is different. I want the computer to work for me first. If I can't make the computer make my life easier, why should I think that my kids would see the need for it?

Granted, I am just in the kindergarten wing. Let me tell you, I had to fight just to make the point that a kindergartner is a real person too. If everyone else gets a computer in their room, so should we. Well, we finally won that battle. Sure, the upper grades got the nice shiny Macintoshes, but they'll get tired of them one day, and they too shall be ours. In the meantime, I am perfectly happy that someone decided that we deserved a machine, and sent me down a perfectly good, albeit slightly scratched up, Apple IIe with an Imagewriter printer. Software? They said, "There's not too much good stuff for that age." Hogwash!

Having lunch a few weeks ago, I edged over to where the computer coordinator (who has never entered my room) placed a pile of discount house software catalogs. You know about those, don't you? If you order from them instead of from the publisher, you can save up to 35% on your purchases. I was looking for a piece of software which would liven up my year-long study of letters...you know, the old "letter of the week" routine that we all do in kindergarten. It really is an effective way to teach the alphabet, and it is so convenient to have 26 letters, almost the same number of weeks, etc. But oh, to make it more interesting!

What I found was not only the perfect program for the old "letter of the week" routine, but also a great introduction for using a real-life computer desktop-publishing tool, and all for the Apple IIe. The name of the program is *Big Book Maker: Letters, Numbers, & Shapes*. What the program does is to provide you with a whole bunch of clip art tools, so that you can make almost any kind of project you want and print it out – all using the concepts from the title.

There are a myriad of ways the program can be used. The clip art includes sections on:

(1) Backgrounds (e.g., Playground, Stage, Toyshelf, Refrigerator)
(2) Frames (Birthdays, City, Shapes, Transportation)

(3) Fonts (Standard, Big, Swirl, Serif, & Fun)

(4) Lots and lots of clip art (Animals, body parts, hats & shoes, giant letters & numbers, and lots more)

When you print out, the program gives you lots of options. If you choose Big Book or Big Big Book, you can print out all the panels of your story or just some. You can also choose to print out in Normal or in Outline form. The Outline option allows you to create coloring books. If you print out normally, and have a color ribbon, it will print out in color.

There is also a Miniature and a Standard option. The miniature will come out like a comic book.

The most obvious thing you can make is a big book. Here's an example of something I did with the kids after I had studied all of the letters and numbers at that point. I had used this program constantly, in a large variety of ways, to help them reinforce the letters and numbers as we learned them. My room was filled with bulletin boards, books, posters, etc., all using this one easy program.

Now, for the end of the year, I told the students that we would be making a classroom alphabet and number big book that we could keep in our classroom library for the children to use next year. The name of the books would be "Our Classroom Alphabet Soup Book" and "Our Classroom Number Theater Book." Using the background "Alphabet Soup," each pair of children, was assigned first to a letter, later to a number. Their job was to use the alphabet soup background, place the clip art letter to which they were assigned on the page, and then to find as much other clip art as they could where the word started with that letter. For instance, one pair had the letter "M." They created their page, then added a monkey, a mouth, a mouse, etc. In addition, I had them create a second page, where they added the ingredients to the soup, using the typing mode. I provided the backdrop - they just had to add words.

My Delicious "M" Soup

1 teaspoon _____

1 tablespoon of _____

Mix in a cup of _____

Add in a _____ and a

pinch of _____

Yum ! Yum!

We did the same for the numbers, only this time we used the "Stage Background," and the students inserted the clip art number (ex. 8), choosing 8 pieces of clip art to surround it.

Teacher Tips:

1. Another piece of software by Toucan Software which works as well is called *Banner Books: All Along The Alphabet.* (Apple II)

2. *Superprint II,* by Scholastic, includes alphabet clip-art. In addition, other clip art disks, available for Macintosh and IBM, can be found with alphabet clip-art.

3. SOFTWARE: *Big Book Maker: Letters, Numbers & Shapes,* Toucan Software (Apple II, IBM, Mac)

Unit Plan

DINOSAURS ARE FOREVER?

Materials

Large dinosaur cutouts, small sturdy cardboard dinosaur cutouts for tracing, chalk, small rubber dinosaurs, collection of dinosaur books (fiction and non-fiction), dinosaur cookie cutters, ingredients for baking sugar cookies, baking utensils, wooden or plastic bones and/or fossils, Apple II computer, color monitor, printer, *Explore-a-Science:Dinosaur Construction Kit: Tyrannosaurus Rex* (William K. Bradford), photo or model of human skeleton, fish skeleton (available at local fish market), poster paints, easel paper, newspaper, paint brushes.

Step One: Preparation

The purpose of this science unit is to help children (preschool to Grade 1) further develop their problem solving skills, physical skills (small and large motor), and language skills. Set the tone for a week of learning about dinosaurs by hanging large cutouts of the various dinosaurs around the room. Become familiar with software program.

Step Two: Non-Computer Activities

- Have children ride their tricycles/big wheels around a life-sized chalk outline of a dinosaur out in the playground.
- Make dinosaur shaped cookies with the children (allow children to do measuring, mixing, cookie cutting, etc.)
- Have cardboard dinosaur cutouts available in art corner for children to trace around.
- During story time, read dinosaur related stories.
- Have rubber dinosaurs available in block area. Children may want to create caves for the dinosaurs.
- Hide plastic or wooden bones and/or fossils in the sand table for the children to excavate. (Be sure to discuss the word "excavate" with the children during circle time.)
- To give the children a better idea of the size of dinosaurs, see how many people it would take to stretch the length of a specific dinosaur.
- Modify "Old MacDonald Had a Farm" to include the names of different dinosaurs. Instead of a duck, Old MacDonald would have a brontosaurus. Encourage the children to imagine what sounds the different dinosaurs might have made.

Step Three: Computer Activity 1

During story hour early in the week, read the storybook that accompanies the software. During Circle time, gather the children around the computer. Remind them about how we carefully put disks into the disk drive that is like a garage and that when the light is on, we never open the garage door. Have one of the students insert the disk, turn the computer and color monitor on. When the program appears, explain that this is just like the story that they had heard earlier, but different. Explain that

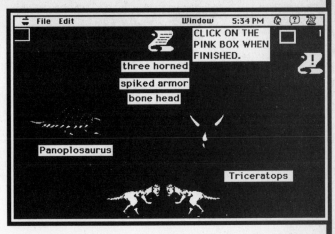

in this story they can make things happen. Demonstrate that using the mouse, they can pick things up and move them around the screen. This will make many things seem to come to life. Discuss the term animate with the children. Follow the story through, having the children take turns uncovering the bones of the dinosaur on the computer screen. Let the children lead the discussion.

Step Four: Computer Activity 2

During a second circle time at the computer, show the children how they can select and add more characters, objects and even words to each screen. Have one of the students use the mouse to move things on the screen and add characters and objects as directed by their peers. With their help, create a short story about dinosaurs. Save it to disk and print it out. Make a copy for each child which they can decorate or color. Be sure to list the children as authors.

Explain to the children that this program will be available on the computer for them to use during the week. Initially, you may need to have an aide or parent helper oversee their work. The children will quickly become adept at using this program.

Follow-Up

As a follow-up activity discuss with the children the skeletal system. Talk about the bones they uncovered in the computer program. Show them a picture of a human skeleton (if possible bring in a model). Discuss their bones and how they can feel them.

Explain that fish have bones, too. Show them a fish skeleton and discuss its structure and how it differs from a human skeleton. Put the fish skeleton on newspaper and have each child first paint it and then take a large piece of easel paper, gently press it onto the fish and take a print of the fish.

111

From The Sidelines

MY FAVORITE SEASON

Wow, am I lucky this year. I'm a sixth grade student at Brophy School. Our teacher, Miss Molliver, told us that each person needed to choose a "civic" project for the year, something that would help out the rest of the school. She gave us lots of choices, but, since I like little kids, I got put into Mrs. Ward's first grade classroom as a "Paired Pal." Everyone knows that Mrs. Ward is the teacher that won that contest last year and got the neatest Macintosh color computer for her class. My mom and dad both have computers at home, so I get to play on them once in a while when they're not working on something important. But Mrs. Ward says that I can help teach the class how to do stuff because she thinks I know more than she does. She also said that if the kids were out at recess, or lunch, that I could use the computer for my own stuff–cool.

Was I in for a surprise when I saw the program that she was having the kids work on when I came for the first time. The program was called *Kid Works 2*. It is one of the greatest things I ever saw. It needs lots of memory, and a color screen, but she has all that. *Kid Works 2* is this program which combines a real easy word processor, a dynamite paint program (a lot like *Kid Pix*, which I love), and this out-of-sight feature where what the kids write can be read out loud right back to them.

The first day I went to the classroom, Mrs. Ward asked me to bring two friends. I brought Chris and Pat. When we got to the classroom, Mrs. Ward had the class together on the rug and was talking to them as a group. They were studying Seasons of the Year, and she had written each season up on the board. She told them to count off by 4's. The 1's were to be in charge of summer. The 2's were in charge of fall. The 3's, winter, the 4's, spring. She assigned each of us big kids to a group, and she took one (because we could write a lot faster than they could). Using that big story chart paper, we had them brainstorm all the things that they could think of that reminded them of each particular season. As the kids called things out, each of us wrote them on the story chart paper. At the end, we taped them all up on the blackboard, and read each other's lists.

Then she began to talk about the plan for the activity. She told them that in their groups, they were to pretend that they had been put in charge of planning a large celebration to honor the beginning of their season. Their job was to plan a story poster that could be displayed which would tell why their season was best, including in their story anything that they particularly liked to do in that season, or anything else that they wanted which would help to advertise it. Since the groups were too large to all work together, she divided the kids into pairs to produce posters.

The best part was when Mrs. Ward showed the kids this software program that they were going to use (with our expert help) to create posters. She decided to do one celebrating our school as an example to show the kids how the program worked. First we created a little story. It went something like this:

CELEBRATE BROPHY SCHOOL

PLEASE COME TO OUR SCHOOL CELEBRATION. WE DO A
LOT OF FUN THINGS AT OUR SCHOOL. WE LEARN TO READ
AND WRITE. WE PLAY GAMES. WE WORK ON A COMPUTER.
WE DRAW PICTURES. YOU WILL HAVE A LOT OF FUN HERE.

Mrs. Ward showed the kids some of the neat features of the program. By clicking an "icon" (an icon is like a picture) of a cat, a whole bunch of the kids' words changed to rebus pictures (there are over 250 of them). By clicking another icon, they change back. By going to a command called "Story Illustrator," the screen changes to a paint program, and the kids can paint a picture which can be placed anywhere in their story. And the neatest part - by clicking on a tape recorder icon, the kids can hear their story read back to them.

So, the job was this: each pair of kids was to try to design their poster story at their seats, (example: Come Celebrate Spring with Me) and then, when it was their time to come to the computer, I helped them to transfer their story and their picture into the computer. I also helped them to save and print and stuff like that. Boy, does this stuff make me feel important. And the kids' posters are great. It really is fun to see these little kids being able to write what they feel, draw things to go with it, and even listen to their story being read out loud to them. This sure beats the old "Write the story and give it to me to correct" that I remember in first grade. Some kids have all the luck. Oh well, maybe my teacher will win the Mac this year.

Teacher Response:

1. This software is available on the Macintosh and the IBM. It is also possible to do this activity using any desktop publishing or graphic program.

2. When working with younger children, help is always wonderful. This lesson describes older students helping out. If you are planning to use the computer a lot, it is also useful to line up a "core" of parent volunteers at the beginning of the year who are willing to sit at the computer as each group of children come up, and help them through the process.

3. SOFTWARE: *Kid Works 2*, Davidson and Associates (Macintosh, IBM)

Lesson Plan

WOOLLY BOUNCE

Purpose

This lesson encourages children (prekindergarten through two) to draw on their natural curiosity to develop thinking and scientific inquiry skills. As they discover the factors that can influence how different balls will bounce, the children begin to learn how to collect data in a scientific experiment.

Materials

Several different kinds of balls (rubber, tennis, basket, golf, volley, bowling, etc.); container for balls; Apple II computer (128K), monitor (color optional), one disk drive; *Woolly Bounce* (MECC); chalkboard and chalk (or easel paper and crayon or magic marker); a small piece of carpet.

Preparation

Become familiar with the components of the software. If you decide to utilize the handout in the teacher's manual, make sufficient copies ahead of time.

Precomputer Activity

Encourage children to discuss any experiences they have had with balls. Show them the rubber ball and ask what would happen if you dropped it onto the hard classroom floor. Ask them to guess how many times the ball will bounce when dropped. Then discuss the concept of prediction. (With older children you may want to see if they can distinguish between guessing and predicting.) After they have made predictions, drop the ball and have them count the number of times it bounces. Ask what would happen if you dropped it onto a floor with a rug. Would it behave differently? Have them make predictions and then count the number of times the ball bounces when you drop it onto the carpet. Compare the number of bounces when it is dropped on the two different surfaces. Display the results on the board.

Show them the tennis ball and ask how many times it will bounce on the hard floor. Record their predictions and then perform the experiment. (Be sure to drop the balls from approximately the same height.) Repeat this exercise on the carpeted floor. Compare results with results of the rubber ball. Do this exercise again, using the basketball. Discuss with the children what makes the balls similar and what makes them different. Contrast the results of the experiments. Show them a bowling ball and have them predict how many times it will bounce. Discuss why you shouldn't bounce it on the floor.

Computer Activity

❶ This exercise can be done as a group exercise or with the children

114

working in pairs. (As a group exercise a large monitor and appropriate hook-up may be necessary, depending upon group size.)

❷ Have a child insert the disk and turn on the computer. At the main menu, choose option 1, "Help Woolly Learn." The second menu allows you to determine the level of difficulty. To begin, choose option 1, "Woolly One." This option allows the children to select only one variable: the type of ball they wish to use. Explain that with Woolly's help, they can see what would happen if the bowling ball were dropped onto the floor. Have a child use the arrow keys to highlight "Ball."

❸ When the menu with the ball choices appears, have a child move the cursor box around the bowling ball and press RETURN to select it. Point out that Woolly is now holding the bowling ball. Next have the child use the arrow key to select "Drop." Encourage the children to count, along with Woolly, the number of times the ball bounces. As the ball is bouncing, the height of the first bounce is recorded on the scale; the number of bounces will be recorded in the box that is resting on the floor. When the ball stops bouncing, have a child press the Space Bar to continue experimenting. Have the children try using a different type of ball, such as a cannon ball or a croquet ball.

❹ With older children, and with children who are familiar with the concept of graphs, you may ask a child to select "Data" from the menu. This allows the child to select one of three data options: a Bounce Graph, a Height Graph, or a Data Chart, as is clearly explained on page 11 in the manual. As children are conducting these experiments, ask them to predict how many times each ball will bounce and how high it will bounce. Which ball will bounce the highest? Which will bounce the least number of times? the most? Ask for predictions about different types of balls. Which kinds of balls will bounce the most? the least? Encourage the children to relate Woolly's experience to their own experiences with balls.

Follow-Up
1. Have *Woolly Bounce* available for the children to use on their own. Encourage them to choose different balls than those done in the large group setting.
2. As a group, choose "Woolly Three." This option will allow you to investigate the difference between dropping the ball on a hard surface versus a soft surface. The children drop the same kinds of balls on both the hard and soft floor, and again make predictions. After they do the experiment, ask them what they learned. Did the balls bounce the same number of times? On which floor did they bounce more? the highest?

From The Sidelines

WELCOME TO US!

Sending my child off to school was so traumatic for me. Not that I haven't spent most of my own life in a classroom, both as a child, and as a teaching adult. I loved teaching, and I now relish teaching my own little one, who is in a prekindergarten classroom. But when the teacher asked me to come in and help on the computer, all of my skills rushed quickly to the back-burner. I taught school in the "pre-computer" generation. How would I get these little four year olds to produce a product? The teacher assured me that, not only was the computer easy to use, but the kids would be much more at ease than I and would lead me along. O.K., says I. How much harder could it be than teaching "to, two and too?"

Thank goodness, Ms. Magnani had the foresight to send me home a copy of the program along with a short written description of what she wanted to do so that I would not be going in "blind." That helped a lot, not only in background but to give me some confidence in what I was doing.

The unit that the students were involved in was a unit about "ME." The software we were going to use was an adorable piece for the Apple II series called *Banner Books: Your School Day*. In it, the students select a number of backgrounds, link them together into a story line, create a "book," and print it out in banner form horizontally. Ms. Magnani explained that our objectives were to: (1) learn to use the software (2) have the children see themselves as a part of a whole group and (3) give them practice with spelling and keying in their names. She explained that there is a fair amount of moving in and out of menus in this program. The management of this would be my task with the children, so that they could concentrate on their decision-making and their creations.

Mrs. Magnani showed me where I would be working. It was a brightly set-up corner marked "Computer Corner." In the corner was an Apple IIGS, and a printer with a color ribbon, all set up and ready to go. On the wall was a laminated wall chart with each child's full name, and their assigned computer time with me (in digital time). Their task was to come at their assigned time, and check their names off with the felt pen when they had done their part.

The morning we started, Ms. Magnani brought all the children to the front rug to explain the jobs for the day, including my learning center - a corner set up in the room with the activity. With a sample of a Banner Book she had previously made, she explained to the children what a Banner Book was. Our class, she said, was going to create a "Banner Book About Us." The children had "work partners" of the week; that is, when there was a group task to be done, Ms. Magnani (who was a big believer in cooperative learning) would pair the children up for that task. The partners changed each week with different kids pairing up, so that their learning experiences would change as well. The children would come up to my Center with their partners at their assigned time, and their tasks would be as follows:

1. Each "page" of the banner would feature Child 1 and his partner, Child 2. Ms. Magnani had picked a classroom background to use for the whole book. Their first job would be (with me to help when needed) to look through the collection of clip art for a character that they wanted to represent them. Some of the clip art showed people; some aliens; some animals. That choice was theirs and theirs alone. The empowerment I saw in each child was most impressive, as they excitedly thumbed through the print-out that Mrs. Magnani had for them, looking for the best character to represent them.

2. Then, with my help, I showed them how to pick a character they liked, and position him/her/it on the screen. Sometimes the two children chose to have their characters interacting. The more they discussed, the richer was the language experience for each of them. Once their clip art was positioned, they were asked to type their names somewhere near their character. That was it, and then on to the next set of children.

The whole process took about 2 hours. Mrs. Magnani had instructed me to leave the first and the last page blank. After hours, she filled in the first page with an introductory "Welcome to a book about us!" She filled the last page with "Come back and see us real soon." The printing was not done during school time - the noise can be very distracting. However, when the project was over, she printed out one large banner for the classroom, and a class set of "miniature" banners for each child to take home.

We all learned a lot. Rachel was proud, not only to have me in the classroom, but also to see Mom learning and enjoying right along with the kids.

Teacher Response:

1. There are other Banner Books available. Some include: *Writing Across America* (American Landmarks), and *All Along the Alphabet*. These are only available for the Apple II computer, but can be used on a Mac LC with an Apple Emulator card.

2. Changing the children's partners on an on-going basis is quite important. Children tend to gravitate towards one or two, which can hinder different perspectives on their learning process.

3. SOFTWARE: *Banner Books: Your School Day* (Toucan Software: Apple only)

Up Front

BEDROOM THEATER

I am so excited about my new Macintosh LC II. Yes, I know they have been around for a while. Yes, I know there are a zillion new models since this one came out–so what? It was only about three years ago that my friend talked me into taking a course over at the Media Center. I was so nervous. What if I broke something? Anyway, the course was great, and the teacher made me realize that (1) it would be very unusual to break something, no matter what I press and (2) there is some neat software out there for my kindergarten children.

I was using an Apple IIe at the time and having a ball watching my class take off with it. I thought I'd have my IIe for life. Then my principal told me I was doing such a great job with technology, he wanted me to try a Macintosh. And I even get new software! I can still use my old Apple II software, because this computer has an emulation card that allows you to run both Macintosh and Apple II software.

The first piece of software I received is this fantastic language arts program called *Storybook Theatre*. Let me tell you about it, and the hundreds of ways to use it with children. There are three "worlds" in which to explore:

    (1)   World 1 is called "In My Room," and is an enchanted room filled with furniture, toys, and imaginary animal friends.

    (2)   World 2 is called "Animal Adventures." This shows a real scene containing animals found in the North American woodlands.

    (3)   World 3 is called "Wacky Scientists." This world is set in a laboratory with two weird scientists doing experiments.

I have used all three with success in my kindergarten room. Worlds 2 and 3 are great, but I'll tell you about only the first world here.

The program is set up as a storyboard, or in "pages." Each page contains less and less information, encouraging the children to add more on their own, both graphics and words. Each world contains five parts–for the kindergarten, I used only the first three.

We started by talking about our own bedrooms and about hiding things there. What did the children hide? Whom did they hide it from? Where were the best places to hide something? This discussion was lots of fun. The children felt like they were "telling secrets," and everyone could get enthusiastically involved. Next, we were ready to look at the software.

On the first page, the complete world is depicted – a boy in a filled room. After briefly showing the whole class how to use the mouse to move things around, I put the children in pairs and gave them time to simply explore. The best practice in oral expression usually happens when the children are left on their own, to share their excitement with each other. To help them along, I gave them a "guide sheet" with ideas. For example: Move the door to see what is behind it...Pick up the fish and put him on the bed... Find 3 objects that do not move... etc.

After all the children had explored page 1, we discussed it as a group. What did you do? What surprised you? What sounds did you hear?, etc. Then I told the children that their next task was to create a room of their own. Page 2 of the storyboard presents a scene with just a background and a "Button Bar" from which to pull characters, objects, etc. One of the features we all love is the recording feature. I can record a direction using the microphone provided with the computer. For instance, when the children clicked anywhere on page 2, they heard me say "Create your own dream bedroom! Hide something somewhere for us to find." Each pair of children created a bedroom. I also told them that if they had time, they could go to the Words Box and look for vocabulary words that would fit into the bedroom.

When the children had created their rooms, we looked once again at just a few of them and tried to find the hidden objects. This part of the lesson was particularly fun for one child in my room, Tim, who has been mainstreamed with Down's Syndrome. Because Tim was not required to read and was virtually in complete control as he created a picture, he met with heartwarming success. He and his partner were able to "fool" us with a carefully hidden frog behind the teddy bear.

The last step was to try writing stories. Page 3 of the Storyboard contains Story Starters. The children read the story starter, and then, by simply opening the Storybook icon, they can type anywhere on the page. The program does not allow for too much of a story; but most first graders don't write that much either! Once they have written in the "textblock," that too can be moved around so that the story can be placed anywhere on the page. The children saved their stories, and we printed them out with a printing option for black/ white outline. This allowed each child to have a story complete with a coloring page at the end.

Both verbal and written expression flourished in the room. The children insisted on going on with other stories, and their ideas were endless.

Teacher Tips:

1. There are several other storybooks in this program. One is called Mr. Murphy's Chowder, and the other is called The Lost Treasures of Zabidonia (all for Macintosh).

2. SOFTWARE used: *Storybook Theater,* Sunburst/WINGS for learning

From The Sidelines

MUPPET LABS

This was my morning to help in my daughter's pre-kindergarten class. I really enjoyed being one of the parent volunteers. I think Emily really enjoyed having Mom join her for the day.

As I entered the room on this fall day I was greeted by Mr. Lyons, the teacher of the pre-kindergarten class. He told me the class was continuing to work on their science project on leaves. He explained that yesterday the children had begun working on making their own leaf booklets. The class had taken a fall walk early in the day and collected leaves, pine cones and other signs of fall. The books that they were making would show all of the different kinds of colorful leaves they had found outside. He told me that the pine cones they had gathered were being stored to be used later to make Thanksgiving turkeys.

As Mr. Lyons guided me over to the computer area, he told me that he would like me to work with the children at the computer. To enhance their work on leaves, they would be working on a program called *Muppet Labs* by Sunburst/WINGS for learning. He told me that he had been working with the program quite a bit and it has a component entitled "Leaf Identification Lab" that would fit right in with what he and the children have been working on.

Emily had followed us over to the computer, so Mr. Lyons asked her to show me how to insert the disk into the Apple II computer and then turn it and the monitor on. The first screen that appeared showed Kermit the Frog going into the Science Hall of Fame. I couldn't help but comment that the children must love the program because of the Muppet characters. Mr. Lyons told me that the WINGS software company offered a number of programs that use the Muppet characters. Unfortunately, he only had this one. I suggested that he give me some information on some of the other programs. Maybe the school's PTA could purchase some of the other software programs.

Emily showed me how to use the arrow keys to make Kermit move from lab to lab. I chose the "Leaf Identification Lab" that had Scooter sitting next to a tree. We then chose Level 1. The manual explained that in Level 1 "students match a leaf to an identical outline in a book."

Scooter holds up a leaf and we have to match it. The arrow keys let us turn the pages to find the matching leaf. When we get the answer right, Scooter smiles at us and puts the leaf on top of the matching outline in the book. When we get the answer wrong, he shakes his head and we get to try again. This was fun. I told Mr. Lyons I thought I could manage this. He assured me that the children would do all of the work. As shown by Emily, they are very comfortable with the computer. My job was just to referee (if necessary) and offer assistance (when necessary). He urged me to have fun with the children and encourage them to talk about what they were doing. Once most of the children had done Level 1, I might want to investigate Level 2

Match the leaf.

with them. In Level 2, the students would have the opportunity to sort different leaves by size, color and shape.

Working with the children that morning was a wonderful experience. It afforded me the opportunity to see Emily's class and teacher in action. I watched as she interacted with the other children and I was especially impressed with the ease with which the children used the computer. It was very clear that I was the novice. Working at the computer seemed to encourage the children to talk with one another and cooperate in problem solving. I was also impressed with how Mr. Lyons had set up the room and the day's schedule. The children moved very easily from one activity area to another. While some children were with me at the computer, others were in the block corner, some were in the Housekeeping area, some were working on their leaf books with the aide, Ms. LeMarche, and some were working with Mr. Lyons making leaf prints with poster paints. The noise level was definitely manageable. The children were learning and most of all were having fun.

Teacher Response:

This science lesson can be linked to a lesson on how things grow. *Learn About Plants* (Sunburst/WINGS for learning) offers a wonderful introduction to how plants grow. While the children are learning how things grow on the computer screen, they can be planting their own seeds and watching them grow.

Up Front

EXPLORING OUR BODIES AND MINDS

What's in a face? Have you ever tried having your students take a good look at other people? What do they see? Are there any two faces alike? In a course at the local university, I played with one program which gave me an idea for having first graders think about just these issues.

A good introduction to this lesson is to bring in a collection of close-ups of people's faces. These can be acquired from magazines, as well as commercial collections that are available in most teacher's supply stores. An alternative here might be for the children to cut their own out, and even make facial expression collections (e.g., smile books, sad books, etc.). Spend some time talking about people's faces in these pictures, and what they say about the person. Imagine what might be going on in each person's life at the moment that picture was taken.

Once I had spent some time talking about the magazine pictures, I introduced the second part of the lesson by talking to my students about facial expressions, and the fact that what your face looks like tells a lot about you. You might want to start by talking about their own facial features:

- What about your face differentiates your face from everyone else's? Here I had the children brainstorm the various features of one's face and put those up on the board (e.g., eyes, nose, ears, hair, etc.).
- Is anyone exactly like anyone else? How do we know that? (One year, I had identical twin boys who looked so much alike that very few of their closest friends could tell them apart at first glance. I had them both stand at the front of the room, and my class gave them the "once over;" that is, what is different, even about them.)

Next, I assigned them a descriptive task. My directions were as follows:

1. Face a partner with a pencil and paper.
2. Look into each other's face, one at a time. One of you is to make an expression of some kind - smile, frown, surprise— anything you want.
3. The partner's job is to describe that person's face as completely as possible.

The children tend to get a little silly doing this, but that's OK as long as I can keep them on task, and keep all descriptions positive. For younger children, you might want to have a worksheet ready for them to use with incomplete sentences such as:

122

My partner's eyes are _____.

My partner's hair is _____ and _____.

My partner's mouth is _____, etc.

I had several children read their descriptions out loud to the class. I then called on one student to read the description while the others kept their eyes closed. See if the class can guess who is being described.

Now we were ready for the computer, so I introduced *Facemaker*. In this program children create a face from scratch. After the face has been created, the program has a lovely component where the children are able to make the face move (e.g., eyes wink, tongue sticks out, nose wiggles, etc.). After showing them in a large group how to create a face, I gave them time over a period of a few days to play with the program, creating a face. For those who cannot read it might be a good idea to make a wall chart behind the computer, indicating the vocabulary words they will need along with picture clues:

MOUTH, EYES, EARS, NOSE, etc.

Once they played with the program, the next step was to teach them how to animate. The program allows the created face to wink, cry, smile, frown, stick out its tongue, and wiggle its ears. Each animation except wiggle (which uses E) uses the first letter of its word. Therefore, this is a good opportunity for listening to beginning sounds. Each action is accompanied by a beginning sound. As a whole group, I had the children cover their eyes and practice listening to a sequence of two, then three sounds, trying to guess what the face is doing.

Last, I let them play a memory game to heighten listening skills. I paired off the students and had each pair create a face of their choice. Then I had one child remain at the keyboard, and the other turn their back to the monitor. Using option two (animation), the child at the keyboard types in a letter that animates the face. The other child listens to the sound that feature makes and must say and demonstrate the action of the *Facemaker* Face. If the action is correctly identified, the children change places.

Kids continued to play the games throughout the school year, on the playground and in the lunchroom.

Teacher Tips:

1. In the programming component, if the sequence moves too fast, typing one or more dashes between the letters slows down the pace.

2. Young children will be able to locate the necessary keys much more readily if you mark the keys with small pieces of colored tape or stickers.

3. NOTE: There is a third component to Facemaker - a memory game, where a sequence of expressions and sounds are given and the student must remember the sequence and type it in correctly.

SOFTWARE: *Facemaker*, Queue, Inc. (Apple II)

Lesson Plan

WE GIVE THANKS

Purpose

This lesson helps students develop speaking, listening, and writing skills while gaining an appreciation for the meaning of the holiday of Thanksgiving. Students will categorize and use key words.

Materials

Muppet Slate, Sunburst/WINGS for learning (Apple)
Seasons and Special Days, Sunburst/WINGS for learning (Apple)

Preparation

Set aside some time a few weeks before Thanksgiving to talk about the history of the holiday. Young children can appreciate the story of the Pilgrims coming to a new country with very little and then building a life, with the constant help of their Native American friends. (For those children who you think are ready, or who live in appropriate communities, a modern day analogy to helping the homeless might be appropriate here.)

Become familiar with the different components of the software programs you will be using. The recommended software is highly motivating and will allow students to both develop skills and take pride in their work.

Precomputer Activity

Using the chalkboard or chart paper, have the children brainstorm some things that they are thankful for. (Possible answers include: food, family, friends, fun, toys, grandparents, school, health.)

Computer Activity

❶ With the children gathered around the computer, put this list into a file on *Muppet Slate.* Review for the children how to start a new file, how to type, etc. If you have access to a classroom TV screen or LCD panel, these would be perfect tools for projecting the list.

❷ Note with the children that everyone is thankful for many items on the list, if they have them. Children, adults, people of different lands, etc., all feel thankful for things like food and clothes and friends. Have the children discuss how to make the list more specific to them. For example:

Who is a person you are especially thankful for?
What food are you most thankful for?
What toy are you most thankful for?, etc.

❸ The final task for the children is to create their own "Thanks for" card to present to their family on Thanksgiving Day. Pick four or five of the general categories that the children have already generated and put them on a wall chart up above the computer. For example:

CATEGORIES FOR GIVING THANKS

1. FAMILY
2. FOOD
3. CLOTHING
4. TOYS
5. YOUR OWN IDEA

❹ Then, depending on the age of the children, do one of the following:

A. For young pre-readers, have a file already set up that looks like this:

1. I give thanks for ...

2. I give thanks for ...

3. I give thanks for ...

4. I give thanks for ...

5. I give thanks for ...

Love,

Using the clip art in either *Muppet Slate* or *Seasons and Special Days,* let the children find one picture to insert in each category. Have the child print out his/ her card, sign it, fold it, and draw a Thanksgiving picture on the front to take home.

B. If the children are ready for beginning writing, they could write their own five sentences, using the rebus pictures if desired, or their own vocabulary. The rest of the procedure is the same.

Follow-Up
1. After students have given their card to their family, have them share with the group some of the responses that they got.
2. Students might work in small groups to prepare seasonal cards in other classes. Encourage the children to discuss ideas for their cards and to work together in creating messages and graphics.

Up Front

ONE-TO-ONE LANGUAGE EXPERIENCES

One of my favorite software series for the Apple II computer is the *Explore-a-Story* series. I think I first developed my real love for it when I heard one of the developers speak about the philosophy behind the series. "Learning is dynamic," he insisted. "Nothing about the learning process is stagnant." So why is it that so much of what we put in front of kids is stagnant? Books, chalkboards, paper tasks... even lots of computer software, all this "still" material, sits in front of active, moving minds. So, why not develop software in which something is always moving? The product: The *Explore-a-Story* series. The series is made up of eight disks. For my kindergarten class, though, my real favorite is *Rosie, the Counting Rabbit.* This is a story of a rabbit who decides to take a walk, and stops to make all kinds of observations on the way. The software package comes with five student books (you can buy more at very little cost) in which the pictures are all computer generated. The real focus of the piece is following Rosie as she takes a walk through her woodsy environment, encountering numbers of things along the way. Each page is a counting page, emphasizing one-to-one correspondence, for example,one cloud/one sun.

Before we begin, I create a set of story characters/objects for the children, similar to what they will see on the screen. Each pair of children is given an envelope containing paper replicas of 1 sun/ 1 cloud, 2 apples/ 2 baskets, etc. Then, as we read and explore the page on the computer, they can match up their cut-up manipulatives on their desks with what they observe on the screen. This provides a wonderful bridge between what they can see and touch and the abstract representation on the computer.

After we have done this activity, reading the story all the way through, I pair the students up, assigning each one a number. Their job is to create a screen of their own (you can do that by clearing an existing screen and using the pictorial menu to bring the scene to life). They then follow the following steps:

1. Pick a screen from the backgrounds section of the menu bar.
2. Pick a number from the objects section of the menu bar (each number is listed as a nice large graphic to be added to a scene.
3. Use either the characters or the objects from the menu bar to create a scene similar to the ones in the book.

For instance, if they have the number 6, they should try to put in 6 bunnies, 6 ducks, 6 lily pads, etc. I also have the children go to the ABC section of the menu, look for the "number word" (six) and put it into the picture. Finally, we print out all of the pictures with the

Rosie counted
_____ _____ .

black & white option, which produces a coloring book effect. Reproducing them as a class set, each child ends up with his/ her own copy of "Rosie's Class Number Book."

There are so many other ways to use this program. Suggestions include:

(1) Have the children create their own Counting Book, modifying each scene of the story as they go along, saving it to disk, and printing it out.

(2) For those children ready to start recognizing and reading beginning vocabulary, the ABC section of the menu is wonderful. I have the children pick their favorite scene of Rosie, and try to pull down and place as many vocabulary words as they can into the picture. Sometimes this may mean adding more pictures themselves from the pictorial menu.

(3) Create "pocket books." If you have a color ribbon on your printer, the *Explore-a-Story* series has a wonderful capability of printing out each scene of the story as a miniature. One of the things I love best about this series is that the kids can read the story over and over again (even if they are non-readers!), modifying it in a different way each time. When they are satisfied with their product, I print their story out in miniature form, laminate it, punch one hole, and string them with yarn. It's wonderful to see them all carry them around in their pockets, comparing "stories" out in the schoolyard.

Teacher Tips:

1. Many of the Explore-a-Stories are also available for the Macintosh.

2. In addition to the *Explore-a-Story* series, there is an *Explore-a-Classic* series (fairy tales), *Explore-a-Folktale* series (folktales), and an *Explore-a-Science* series, all written on the same model.

3. Several versions of the software are available from William K. Bradford Publishing, including: *Explore-a-Story: Rosie the Counting Rabbit,* (Apple II) and *Explore-a-Story Plus: Rosie the Counting Rabbit* (Mac version)

Unit Plan

MOSAIC MAGIC

Software Description

When busy teachers look for software, they often refer to catalogs of publishers they know. A teacher might purchase items sight-unseen, based on the reputation of the publisher. This might be a "safe" way to go in some cases; in other cases, the results will be disappointing. One award-winning program in a catalog does not mean that another program will be equally rewarding. So going strictly with the large "conglomerate" companies, you could miss a real gem. One such gem is *Mosaic Magic*. The company (Kindermagic Software) is small, but mighty in ideas. The program is one of only four that was written up in the early childhood section in one of the most reputable review publications, *Only the Best - 1993 Edition*.

Mosaic Magic is a program where children discover patterns and develop problem solving skills in the process. The mosaics provide important pre-math work in pattern and shape recognition. Children love this imaginative and versatile program, and it provides wonderful help for you, the teacher, in preparing materials. The program is made up of three components:

(1) Tattle Tiles: This is a "what-is-missing" type of puzzle activity. The screen displays a mosaic pattern or picture with one or more missing tiles, marked by smiling stars. The player's job is to fill in these stars by choosing a tile or tiles of the correct shape and color to complete the picture. There are three levels of difficulty to the game.

(2) Copy Cat: A picture is shown on half of the screen (horizontal or vertical). The other half of the grid is used to copy the picture. The difficulty level is selected from the level pop-up window. To help find where to place the tiles, smiling stars appear where the picture is to be copied. There is a help tutorial if the child places wrong three times.

(3) Masterpieces: This is an artistic exploration that encourages children to design their own pictures using the many shapes and colors of mosaic tiles available. The child can start from scratch, or can choose from twenty "Picture Starters" on the disk.

Classroom Activities

There are many ways that the program can be used in the classroom. Most of these ideas would presume that the children first spend time playing the first two games, both to gain proficiency in the program and to "warm up" to working with patterns and shapes. Examples:

- Have the children create a holiday mosaic card to take home. You can do this for any holiday, with the children writing a greeting on the back of the card. (Preschoolers can be encouraged to spell their names, with help.)

- Have two children work together to create a "half" of a picture. Save this, and let another pair try to create the other half to be identical. This activity could be completed on or off the computer.

- You can use *Mosaic Magic* yourself to create some wonderful games for the children. Use the tool program to make a game, then print it out and duplicate it. You can use this program for games such as dominoes, concentration, bingo, and lots more.

- Using designs the children have created, transfer the designs to the special paper used to make T-shirts. Children will proudly wear their interesting mosaic designs for month. Tape each design to cardboard. Then place the designs side by side on a large bulletin board. The result will be most impressive.

- If children are a little older (first grade or above), you might foreshadow work on coordinates by giving them a marked grid and a set of directions for placing certain squares in certain places. If they follow your directions correctly, the children will end up with a picture of a sailboat, a Halloween pumpkin, a tree, or other fun and motivating choices.

- If you are studying transportation, have each child create a mode of transportation. If you are studying animals, have the children create that animal using mosaics. Display the children's work.

As the children explore the many creative possibilities in the program, it is also important for them to have real mosaic tiles to manipulate. By moving comfortably back and forth between the actual tiles and the symbolic representations on the computer, the children will have a truly integrated learning experience.

Software

Mosaic Magic, Kindermagic Software (*Macintosh or IBM*).
Other software that would work well with this unit: *Patterns & Seqiences*, Hartley Software (AppleII), or *Patterns*, MECC Software (Apple II)

Lesson Plan

MUPPET MATH

Purpose
This lesson will help children (PreK-1) realize that math is everywhere. It will develop students' counting skills and introduce them to the concept of graphs. The concepts of most and least will be reinforced.

Materials
Apple II computer (or Macintosh LC with Apple emulator card and 5 1/4" disk drive); regular keyboard, Muppet Learning Keys, or Touch Window. Color Monitor is recommended. *Muppet Math* (Sunburst/WINGS for learning). Laminated ten-strip, blocks for markers, paper eyes made from construction paper, easel paper, tape.

Preparation
Become familiar with the software program. Explain to the gym teacher (if gym is a separate program) the concepts you will be developing so that these can be incorporated into gym activities. Secure the ten-strip to the floor of the gym area. Print out pictures of simple graphs from *Muppet Math*.

Precomputer Activity
During physical education, have one of the children walk along the ten-strip as the other children count aloud. Have a child pick a number on the ten-strip and stand at that point. Have another child walk along the strip until he/she reaches the first child. The children should be counting out loud as the second child walks to meet the first child.

Have the children choose an exercise, such as deep knee bends, toe touching, sit-ups, etc. Ask a child to choose a number and place a block on it. Have the children do the chosen exercise the number of times indicated by the number chosen, counting out loud. Repeat this format for several other exercises. Be sure to leave markers in place along the ten-strip.

Have children gather around the ten-strip and look at the markers on it. What does it show them? Which exercises did they do the most? Which did they do the least? Using pictures of simple graphs, explain that the ten-strip is like a bar graph showing how many times they did each exercise.

Computer Activity
❶ Gather the children around the computer. When the Main Menu appears, have a students move Kermit to the Gymnasium. (Elicit that context clues tell which room is the Gymnasium.)

❷ The next screen will show Miss Piggy waiting to do her exercises. Have a child decide how many jumps Miss Piggy should do and enter the number into the computer. Point out that as Miss Piggy is jumping, the graph at the top of the screen is becoming shaded. The shaded line is moving along the number strip matching the number of jumps she makes.

❸ If your students give the correct answer, Miss Piggy will follow their instructions. If their answer is incorrect, the screen will guide them to the correct answer. When Miss Piggy has done the appropriate

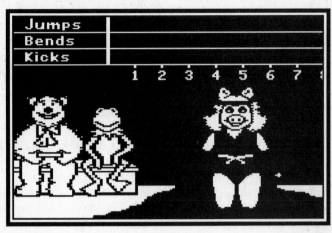

number of jumps and your students indicate that she should do no more, she will curtsey and Kermit will applaud her. Show the children that the graph is now shaded to match the number held by Fozzie. Continue by having Miss Piggy do her bends and kicks.

❹ Make the program available to the children during free time. You or a helper should be available for guidance when necessary. Set the program to Level 2. The game is played the same as in the first activity, but the computer will ask "how many more?" The children must enter the correct missing number, encouraging them to find missing addends.

Follow-Up

Explain to the children that they are going to help you create a graph to show the different color eyes in their class. On large easel paper, write the header: <u>EYE COLOR</u>. Along the left side of the paper, write the words *brown, gray, blue,* etc. Next to each word, put a colored construction paper eye in the appropriate color. Then have each child choose a paper eye that matches his/her eye color. Demonstrate by putting up an eye to match your eye color. Have the children, one at a time, paste their paper eye next to the matching eye on the chart. When everyone has had a turn, have the children discuss the graph they have created. What does it tell them? Are there more people in the class with blue eyes or brown eyes? Talk with the children about other things graphs could be about. Have supplies in the craft area in case they wish to make their own graphs.

From The Sidelines

OUR EVER-CHANGING BODIES

To be a principal is to know to expect the unknown. So I had come into Mrs. Garcia's room not quite knowing what to expect. She told me that they had been studying the human body, and that I should come and see some of the ways she had incorporated the computer into what she had done. Naturally, I was more than a little skeptical. After all, what could she possibly get a bunch of 5 and 6 year old kindergartners (many of them bilingual) to do on a computer?

The whole room was divided into learning centers, and each center seemed to represent a different part of the body. They were colorfully decorated, and full of children's work. Prominent in the room was only one computer, an Apple IIGS, but it was set up in such a fashion, that you could see it from anyplace in the room. Next to it was an Imagewriter II printer, which was busily printing out with two very excited youngsters watching its progress. I decided that the best way to really see everything was to request a student "tour guide." So off we went, Carlos and I.

Center #1: OUR TEETH

Most children of this age have a fascination with their teeth. Carlos explained that a dentist came to the classroom to visit. She brought lots of interesting information which was colorfully displayed at the Center for children to "read." Then Carlos showed me how Mrs. Garcia, as a follow-up, had made a chart divided by months for each child in the class. Then, according to Carlos, using the *Super Science Activity Shop,* they had printed out a set of "clip art" teeth for each child, and placed them in an envelope next to their chart. When someone lost a tooth, they had to figure out which one it was, cut and paste it on his/her chart. Carlos said that they often had to look in a mirror to really see which tooth they lost.

Center #2: WHAT WE EAT

This Center was located near the classroom cooking center. Carlos explained that they had talked about what kinds of foods they liked, what they did not like, and lastly, what they had never tried. Then, using the software program again, Mrs. Garcia printed out a lot of the food "clip art."

Each child got a set of clip art and a piece of paper divided into 4 sections. The sections read like this: MEATS I LIKE, VEGETABLES I LIKE, FRUITS I LIKE, GRAINS I LIKE. The children used the clip art, cutting and pasting foods according to their own tastes. Then, Carlos said, they all compared their charts before putting them on the wall. Lastly, there was a large class chart entitled FOODS WE TRIED. Carlos said that, every other day, Mrs. Garcia helped them prepare a food with which they were not familiar. Then the children would find that food on the clip art, cut it out, and put it on the appropriate side - I LIKED IT, I DIDN'T LIKE IT - with their names underneath!

Center #3: WATCH US GROW

This Center had two big displays. First, there were two giant skeletons on the wall, all made from "clipart" from the *Super Science Activity Shop*. Carlos explained that the teacher had shown the class, using the computer, each of the major bones in the body. They printed them out in "mega-size," and put them together on the wall. Carlos said it took a very long time to print out in that size, but it was worth it to see it put together.

The other half of the Center had a great wall chart ruler - also printed out from the *Super Science Activity Shop*. Each child picked a different color crayon, which would become his/her crayon for the year. Then using the ruler to measure themselves against the wall, Carlos said that they each took a partner and measured themselves, writing their names next to their measurement marks. Carlos said that Mrs. Garcia was going to let them do it three more times during the year, and that this wall chart would stay up until the end of the school year.

Well, my tour was over, and was I ever impressed. All of this work had been done by a group of young children, using just one computer and one simple program. Mrs. Garcia shared with me later that there were even more things you could do with this program – it was so versatile. She also said that it was particularly helpful for some of her bilingual youngsters in terms of building vocabulary – a helpful bonus.

Teacher Response:

1. What my principal got: I was so pleased to see that what I had tried to achieve really showed. I get tired of my early childhood colleagues telling me that they cannot use this or that piece of software, because the kids "couldn't handle it."

2. What my principal missed: From the way he described Carlos' tour, it sounds like I worked months on these centers. In fact, this program was so easy that I had the Centers and the directions set up in one afternoon after school. The manual for this program is easy to follow, and meant for the novice!

3. Software source: *Super Science Activity Shop*, Scholastic (Apple).

Up Front

SILLY NOISY CLASSROOM

Some of my favorite activities with my young students are in the field of sensory awareness. Perhaps that is because they always enjoy it as much as I. It is well documented that children of this age learn best when you begin with "the self" and move on to the outside world in older years. Piaget certainly said that, in encouraging us as teachers to move from the concrete (there is nothing more concrete than our own bodies) to the abstract (other people's bodies). In the field of computer education, Seymour Papert, a researcher at MIT, developed the LOGO programming language with the philosophy that if children were taught from the basis of their own experiences, they would learn the best.

In his book, *Mindstorms,* Papert referred to his own childhood fascination with "gears." He had a lot of trouble learning, except when it was something he could relate to his knowledge of the way gears work. Once he could establish a relationship to that, other more abstract concepts became much easier for him to understand.

To take this down (or up?) to the early childhood level, young children do not have to be taught to smell, to see, to hear, etc. (except in very unusual circumstances). These are bodily functions that the majority of us take for granted. They are also skills to which we as teachers can do much to heighten sensitivity! I will list a few activities which I would do with my children off the computer to introduce a series of lessons on sensory awareness.

SIGHT

To show how much we depend on our eyes, a classic exercise is the blindfold. With young children, play the children's birthday game "Pin the Tail." You can easily adapt this to whatever you are studying. If you are studying The Ocean in social studies, for example, play "Pin the Fin on the Fish." The point here is to show them how hard it is to get around without our eyes. Have them discuss how it felt to move around blindfolded.

HEARING

One game my children always like is the "Do You Hear What I Hear?" There are many good records available for this as well, but you can do it with simple classroom sounds. Have them put their heads on their desks or tables (no peeking!) and ring a bell, move the eraser across the chalk-board, tap a pencil, etc.

SMELL

Again a classic exercise and one which the children love is the Mystery Boxes. Take a set of small boxes with lids, fill each one with some smell with which the children are familiar, put a small hole in the top for their noses, and play. I fill them with things like cinnamon, orange peel, chocolate, peanut butter, banana, etc. Spices and food flavoring work well here!

TASTE

One thing which my primary children are not clear on at all is the difference between sour and bitter, salty and sweet. They know it when they taste it, but have trouble expressing it. This exercise is a lot of fun, and I particularly enjoy their little faces when it doesn't taste so great! Using very small amounts of an appropriate food for each taste bud, have the children close their eyes, and place the food on their tongue. Then, have them describe what they taste. Have them come to a cooperative consensus on the right vocabulary word to describe it - this sometimes leads to interesting discussions!

FEEL

An activity similar to the mystery boxes (Smell) can be done here. Again, fill cardboard boxes with different textures (satin, plastic, pine cone, cotton, etc.). Make sure that you put in a few ringers - slime, putty, etc. Put a hole in these boxes big enough for a small arm to fit in. Let them reach in and watch the reactions!

Once you have done a number of these off-computer activities, have a whole class discussion about senses in their homes. Put the five senses on the board and, under each one, have the children brainstorm as many things as they can think of which relate to their home. What do they hear? What do they see? What can they feel? I find that this brainstorming session works very well when I "set the atmosphere." That is, I turn my lights down, have the children lie on the floor in the front of the room, close their eyes, and pretend they are in their favorite room in their house. After they tell which room that is, have them do this brainstorming. When I teach, I find that anything that "changes the scene" for them evokes more response!

Next, I ask the children how many have a playroom in their home. If they do, we talk about their playrooms in terms of their five senses. What can they hear in there? What can they feel? Of course, depending on the economic status of those that you teach, be careful to be sensitive to those who may not be lucky enough to have a play area. However, all children play, some with expensive toys, some with whatever they can put together. Therefore, this can be easily adapted to using the five senses with their playthings. Another way to adapt might be to use the housekeeping center which most primary teachers have in their classrooms. Transform it for the duration of this activity into a "Playroom," and use their experiences from there!

Up Front (cont.)

Lastly, I ask the children to imagine a room where everything did something! No matter what they did, they get a response. This is a lead in, then, to showing them *The Playroom* by Broderbund. This is a multi-sensory program

where, no matter what the children click, something will happen. They click on the bird, it will warble. They click on the nightstand drawer, it opens with a squeak and a balloon floats out (which will eventually pop). Some things the children click on produce more than a single event; they open up a game. For instance, there is an ABC Book on the bookshelf. When that is clicked on, a castle scene opens up and the children can create their own fairy tale. A mouse hole opens up a board game.

This program (or one of the alternatives listed) can be used in many different ways with the children.

(1) My students always liked doing it together as a class the first time, with different volunteers coming up to choose something to click. We would watch and then discuss (1) what was the action taken and (2) which of the five senses did it employ. This was an excellent culminating activity to our lesson/ unit on the senses.

(2) It can be used by pairs of pupils who sit at the computer, and take turns trying out the different parts of the scene. In this case, I would provide them with an accompanying activity sheet to fill in. Depending on the age, one could replicate pictures from the screen and have the children match the picture to the sense which most matched it.

(3) I found that although the activities and the motions do not change, the children did not tire of playing this over and over again. Why? Because, I feel, a truly quality software program puts the control as much as possible in the hands of the user. The program facilitates learning, but does not dictate it! I think that definition applies to quality teaching as well! A child who feels that they can control the direction in which they are going on a program will gain a much richer understanding of the role of technology in their lives.

Another wonderful feature about using this program with very young children is the fact that there is no "right or wrong." I find that even my 3 year olds, given minimal direction, are learning quickly and proficiently how to use the mouse - unlike their more "fearful" adult partners! Therefore, this is a program that the children can use with little or no help.

To culminate the lesson(s), after the children are thoroughly familiar with the program, use it as a whole class again, having them share with each other which aspects of the room they liked the best and why. Finally, you might want to bring them "back to the concrete" by having them draw their own playrooms at home. Each child should be ready to share their playroom, and explain for each component of their drawing what it is, and what "sense" it evokes. Great bulletin board material!

The alternate software listed below works just as well. The *McGee* series is also completely experiential, as McGee and his friends move around in their environment. The only real difference is that the variety of responses is not as varied; that is, no games, just picture actions.

The *Silly, Noisy House* is similar to *The Playroom*, except it is on CD-ROM. Therefore, the cause/effect actions are greatly enhanced, taking advantage of the extra power.

It should be noted that the Macintosh version of *Playroom* and *Treehouse* also take advantage of the "Recording" feature on the Mac LC. Using the microphone, you can record a direction, a quick "hello," a "Happy Halloween" on any object on the screen. This opens the door for a plethora of other exciting possibilities in oral language. Think about it!

Teacher Tips:

GRADE LEVEL: K-1

SOFTWARE: Choice of : *Playroom*, (Broderbund), *Treehouse*, (Broderbund), *Silly, Noisy House* (CD Rom, Voyager) *McGee, McGee at the Fun Fair, Katie's Farm*(Lawrence Productions).

Lesson Plan

MUPPETS ON STAGE

Purpose

This lesson helps children (PreK-K) learn to recognize the letters of the alphabet while developing computer skills. Concrete activities are provided to help children "learn by doing."

Materials

Computer (Macintosh, Apple II or MS-DOS), color monitor, two disk drives, Muppet Learning Keys if available (for Macintosh, Apple, or MS-DOS depending on available computer), *Muppets on Stage* (Sunburst/WINGS for learning); paper bag filled with objects or pictures for the letter of the day; books related to the alphabet (see Note); supplies for making books (see Additional Activities).

Preparation

Become familiar with the software program. For the letter of the day, provide a number of objects or pictures of objects familiar to children: apple, picture of an alligator, book, ball, etc. Place a collection of alphabet books in the book corner, and choose several books to read during story hour.

Precomputer Activity

Introduce the letter of the day during circle time. Take from the paper bag different objects or pictures and ask the children to identify them. Elicit or tell the children that they all begin with the same letter. Have the children suggest other words that begin with that letter. Then, if possible, read a book related to the letter.

Computer Activity

❶ Explain the Muppet Learning Keys to the children and let them experiment with the keys. If the Muppet Learning Keys are not available, show the children the regular keyboard and discuss the different keys.

❷ The first screen will show the three stages that you and the children can choose. "Discovery" will help the children become familiar with the program and the use of the Muppet Learning Keys. "Letters" encourages the children to match either a lower case or upper case letter to the corresponding letter on the keyboard. In "Numbers" the children are asked to correctly count the number of objects on the screen.

❸ Have a child select "Letters." The screen that appears will show five pedestals. A letter will appear on the large white pedestal in the middle of the screen. Have a child press the corresponding letter on the keyboard. If the answer is correct, the result will be an animated sequence. An incorrect answer will prompt a sound and the child can try again.

❹ Once each child has had an opportunity to try the program, have the children move on to other activities around the room. Tell them that they can try the program again whenever they like during free activity time.

Follow-Up

Choose the "Discovery" stage and let the children explore. This portion of the program will present them with an empty stage with easels on both sides of the screen. When a child presses a letter on the keyboard, an object beginning with that letter will appear. If the child presses a number, a corresponding number of objects will appear. The children can change the colors by pressing a color on the paint box on the Muppet Learning Keys. The children will have fun discovering all the things they can make happen.

Additional Activities

Have the children make their own letter books. Have construction paper or oak tag cut into 4" x 6" pieces. As each letter of the alphabet is introduced to the children, give them a piece of this paper to form a new page. On this page, they should print the letter of the day. (For those children having difficulty forming letters, you may wish to provide tracing materials.) Have the child put a picture on the page to match the letter of the alphabet. Pictures can be either stickers, clippings from magazines, or drawings by the children. Once the children have worked through the alphabet, they can punch holes in the pages and use ribbon, yarn, or string to hold them together. (As the children are working on their pages, remind them to put their name on the back of each page.)

Notes

1. You might look for the following books in the library: *ABC An Alphabet Book* photographed by Thomas Mattresen, *Frederick's Alligator* by Easter Allan Peterson, *Alligators All Around* by Maurice Sendak.
2. This exercise is most effective with young children when *numerous* alphabet objects are used.

From The Sidelines

NUMBER FUN

Working with numbers and number concepts can take all kinds of forms at the early childhood age, particularly when the children are in nursery school and kindergarten. The more different approaches and styles used to present the concepts to the children, the more they will come to understand what is being presented.

Trying to develop a true understanding of what the numbers from 1 to 10 represent is a good part of the mathematics curriculum at the very early childhood level. As we all know, and as critics of the computer at a young age are quick to point out, children must and should work with concrete manipulatives at this age. They must be able to feel, to touch, and to observe what the number "3" means in order to bridge that gap from concrete to abstract thought. Therefore, as we try to emphasize throughout this book, the computer should not replace the work with manipulatives; rather it should sit alongside the manipulatives as an enhancement and enricher of the concrete tasks in which the children are taking part. The computer can help to serve to bridge that gap from concrete to abstract. It presents the manipulatives on the screen, abstract representations of what the children may indeed have played with that day. The teacher's job is to make those representations "match" what else is going on in the classroom so that the connection for the students is clear and natural. There are several ways in which technology can help in this endeavor.

One program which can be used to practice number concepts is the "Discovery" section of *Muppets on Stage. Muppets on Stage* has three parts: the Discovery part, a letters practice, and a numbers practice. The latter two are fine for review; the first section however, is much richer in creativity and student-oriented learning. It is strictly what the title suggests: a "discovery." Ideally, the child would be working with an alternative keyboard called the "Muppet Learning Keys" when working with this software. The "Keys" provides an environment for the young child with which they are more familiar. Letters are in alphabetical order; numbers appear on a ruler; to "erase" is on a real eraser; colors are on a paint palette, and so on. Sunburst/WINGS for learning produces these keyboards - they also have made sure that all of their early childhood programs are compatible.

When the child presses a "V," a violin appears. When he presses an "8," 8 violins appear. When he presses "GO" (the equivalent of return) the violins start playing a song. Each letter has its own pictures, and actions. So, if you are working on numbers, you could create any number of directionality tasks, using this program. Have the children work in pairs and follow these directions. Examples:

Make 3 zippers move.

Make 7 yo-yos bounce.

Make 4 fires burn.

The next step is to have the children create representations of the numbers for display around the room. Using *Print Shop*, they can create "Number Posters." Each pair of children is assigned to a number. Their job is to use the program to print a number, and then a set of graphics (clip art) to represent that number. If you are working with the nursery school set, you can have a parent or teacher aide work with the children on this; however, you will be surprised at how much they can pick up on their own. Of course, each group has to agree on the graphics to be used. This can become, especially for some of our more "strong-willed" tots, a great lesson in cooperative learning.

When the posters are finished, they can be placed around the room in order, much cheaper and more creative than the store-bought variety.

Another use of *Print Shop* would be to create number banners. Print the "1," then a picture to go with it, next the "2," then two pictures with that, and so on till 10. A great experience for them (albeit a distracting one) is to then print it out for the kids to watch. Banners take a long time to print out. It can become a great experience in computer literacy, as well as predicting, etc. to hypothesize on what is taking so long, what is the computer doing when it is "thinking" - as the screen suggests, etc.

As the year goes on, if the students are ready, *Print Shop* can be used to illustrate simple number sentences, or as a way of integrating holiday and math activities (e.g., How many Santas are on this poster; Count the hearts on this valentine card, etc.)

The combination of these two early childhood programs can do much to enrich your preschool mathematics curriculum.

Teacher Response: _____

There are many alternatives to Print Shop on the market. Any program which creates signs and banners is acceptable for this lesson. These are available for Apple, Mac, and IBM, and may even be found in public domain. SOFTWARE mentioned includes *Muppets on Stage*, (Sunburst/WINGS for learning: Apple, Mac, IBM), and *Print Shop*, (Brøderbund:Apple, Mac, IBM)

Up Front

JUST GRANDMA AND ME

"Bye, Mom. See you after school," I called as I ran into my classroom. "Hi, Mrs. Kaufman. I'm here."

"Good morning, Rachel. Are you ready for a busy day?" Mrs. Kaufman asked.

"Yup. Mrs. Kaufman, since I'm the first here, can I read about Grandma on the computer?"

"Of course you can. Come help me set it up."

I love to use the computer. Mrs. Kaufman reminded me that the little box next to it is a CD player. We put the CD with Little Critter's picture on it into the box. When Little Critter appeared on the screen, Mrs. Kaufman asked me if I wanted to have the story read to me or if I wanted to play. I decided I wanted to play.

As Mrs. Kaufman left the music began. This was going to be fun. I told Joelle she could play too when she came into the class. We both watched Grandma and Little Critter come out of their house and go down the walk. When they got to the road we heard Little Critter say, "We went to the beach, just Grandma and me." When the little arrow came back on the screen I knew that I could make things happen.

"Joelle, watch what happens when I point to the mail box!" I moved the mouse so that the little arrow was pointing to the mail box. When I pushed the mouse button down, the door of the mail box opened up and a lot of water and a frog fell out! Did we ever laugh.

"Hey, that's neat," yelled Timmy, who had just come into the room. "What else does something?"

"Oh, I can make almost everything do something," I bragged.

"What happens when you point to the hole in the tree?" asked Joelle. "I wonder if anyone lives in there?"

Other people came up to the computer to see what we were doing.

"I bet a bird lives in there," said Peggy.

"Birds don't live in holes, stupid," said Jason.

"Let's find out," I said, and I pointed to the hole. We watched a squirrel poke his head out of the hole and run all around the tree.

"Hey, where did he go?" asked Timmy.

"He went back into the tree," Peggy answered.

Next I pointed to the front door of the house. We heard the doorbell ring, but no one came to the door. "That's because no one is home," said Joelle. "Let me point to the window so I can see what happens."

Joelle grabbed the mouse and pointed to the window. The telephone rang! Next we heard the answering machine, so we knew that no one was home. "Hey, we have one of those at our house!" Timmy said.

"So do we," said Jason. "It has a real funny message that my brother made."

I pointed to the little arrow down in the corner while everybody else was talking about answering machines. They all shut up real quick when they heard a horn beep. We watched a bus came up the road and stop in front of Grandma and Little Critter. They climbed on the bus and the screen got dark. A little man walked across and then we were on page two.

Mrs. Kaufman kept an eye on the growing group over in the computer area. She had been a little hesitant when she heard about Brøderbund's new *Living Books*. She wasn't sure if children would reap the same benefits from seeing a book read on the computer to hearing someone read it. As she watched the children using the CD *Just Grandma and Me*, she realized that this animated storybook was involving them in many different ways.

It was a wonderful tool for the whole language approach to teaching word recognition and beginning reading skills. And the children were learning cooperatively while making use of their newfound problem solving skills. The program also offered ESL opportunities since the story could be heard in Spanish or Japanese. This was an interesting format. She was glad she had decided to give this versatile program a try. The results exceeded anything she had imagined.

Teacher Tips:

The *Living Book* series is a dynamic tool for use in a whole language classroom. *Just Grandma and Me* can be used to introduce a lesson on the ocean and its inhabitants. If you live near the ocean, encourage the children to talk about their experiences when they visited the beach. For children who have never been to the ocean, this can serve as an introduction to its wonders. This particular story also offers an excellent opportunity to help young children distinguish between real and make-believe. Do starfish really dance? Do they dance with a hat and a cane? The possibilities are endless.

Lesson Plan

MYSTERY OBJECTS

Purpose

This lesson will help children (PreK-1) draw on their natural curiosity to develop thinking skills. Children will identify hidden objects by learning about the different attributes of these objects. Activities provide an opportunity for children to develop skills in observation, communication, classification, and comparison.

Materials

Apple II computer, *Mystery Objects* (MECC 1988), printer, printer paper, chalkboard or easel paper, chalk or magic marker, large brown paper bag, objects with different attributes.

Preparation

Gather a group of objects with different attributes (size, texture, temperature, sound, etc.). Take the time to try out the software program and look over the manual.

Precomputer Activity

During circle time, have the children talk about how they are alike and how they are different. For example, they are alike in that they all have eyes; they are different in that their eyes might be blue, brown, or green. Ask the children to think of many ways in which they are alike and different. Then explain what an attribute is: a quality that belongs to a person or thing. One attribute of a ball is the fact that it is round; an attribute of a flower is its fragrance. Encourage the children to think of other familiar objects and name their attributes.

Take this to the concrete level with a hands-on experience. Put a mystery object into a large brown paper bag. Ask a child to reach into the bag and without looking try to determine what the object is. After one child has touched the object, have another child smell it. Have a third child pick up the bag to see how heavy the object is. Encourage the children to verbalize their findings, and record these on the chalkboard or easel paper. Read back what the children have reported and ask them to figure out what the object is. When the children have guessed (or made deductions), ask them to give reasons for their answers. Then show them the object so they can see if they are correct.

Computer Activity

❶ Connect your computer to a large monitor (if available) or gather the children around your computer. The Main Menu will provide you with four options. Choose "Information" and go over the instructions with your students. Explain to them the six different attribute finders (tools):

> Funny-Feeler
> Sizer-Upper
> Heavy-Holder
> Super-Sniffer
> See-Shaper
> Color-Seeker

❷ Discuss what each of these tools can find out about an object. Explain to the children that they are going to see four different objects and then one will be hidden. It will be their job, with the help of the tools, to figure out which object has been hidden.

❸ Proceed to "Practice Sessions" and give the children the opportunity to identify a mystery object that is hidden among other objects. The other objects displayed on the screen will have very different physical traits than the mystery object. Hints are available if the children need a little help.

❹ Let each child have a turn at the computer. Encourage the other children to offer suggestions and advice. Once you feel confident that the children understand the program, move onto "On Your Own." With younger children, start out at the easy level. You may wish to call on student volunteers to help guide the class in identifying the hidden objects.

Follow-Up

Additional classroom activities, such as using a Mystery Box, are suggested in the manual that accompanies the software, beginning on page 18. This software is a wonderful lead-in to a discussion on individual disabilities such as blindness. Check out *Books About Handicaps for Children and Young Adults: The Meeting Street School Annotated Bibliography* (The School, 1978).

Notes

1. *Mystery Objects* offers a variety of Teacher Options that enable the teacher to work with individual student's records as well as edit the program's settings.
2. This program has correlation for older children using the following textbook series: Scott, Foresman; Addison-Wesley; Merrill; Silver Burdett & Ginn; Coronado Press, Inc.

From The Sidelines

NAME BANNERS

I love going in to observe in Mrs. Kingsbury's Happy Hollow Nursery and Kindergarten. No matter what time of the day, no matter when in the year I decide to pop in for "an early childhood fix," the place is bustling with excitement: children busily working at any number of different learning centers, and everyone well-directed and involved in their individual tasks.

The other reason that I love to visit Happy Hollow is that Mrs. Kingsbury is one of those "adventurous souls" who has not been afraid to bring the computer in, not only to her kindergarten students, but even to her tiny three year olds. The children love it. The teachers, of course, were the ones who needed a little prodding. "Why use the computer with students this young?" they asked. What could these little ones, who need to be so involved in the world of concrete and manipulatives, gain from an abstract medium like the computer?

These teachers were in for a shock. I had observed the children several times over the course of the year, trying out simple ABC and number programs, generally getting used to the keyboard as they got used to the other classroom routines. Not only did the children take to the machine right away, but it quickly became the most sought after "Center" in the room. Cooperative learning and sharing took place more naturally there than in any other area of the room. Each time I came in, I observed that the children were more and more comfortable with their computer tasks - even the teachers seemed to relax.

This particular day, I came in and decided to watch the kindergartners, who were going to do a computer activity. Mrs. Kingsbury has worked hard at getting computers and software for her school. Just this year, she applied and got a mini-grant which bought her a Macintosh LCII, and a small collection of software to go with it. She was thrilled, and so were her students, many of whom had worked on the Apple II in the nursery last year.

The children had been working on beginning sounds, and alphabet recognition. Using *Superprint* for the Macintosh, Mrs. Kingsbury told the children that their task was going to be making "Name Banners." She divided the children into pairs. Their task was to look through the vast collection of clip art (all the pictures are shown in the back of the documentation), and find one picture

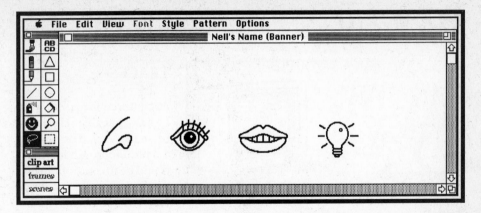

whose beginning sound matched each letter of their name. So, for instance, Kit might have pictures as follows:

K – kangaroo
I – ice cream cone
T – toaster

Mrs. Kingsbury taught the children how to create a banner, by making one together with them in class - saying the words "HAPPY HOLLOW." Each pair of students was given one period of time to work on their banners. It was wonderful to watch the two children pore over the documentation, looking for just the right pictures for their special project. Of course, each was more than willing to help the other, taking great excitement in each one's finished product.

Once they had created both banners, the children called Mrs. Kingsbury over to save it for them. I was so impressed in their ability to work most of the program through by themselves. I think they were impressed as well!

As a banner was created and printed out, Mrs. Kingsbury taped it up. I was able to come back and visit a few weeks later and, oh, the room was filled with computer print-outs - each proudly displaying the name of the artist. Back to school night for this school would certainly be impressive.

Teacher Response:

1. Printing takes a long time, particularly if you are making a banner. I believe it is very smart to do it after school; the sound of the printer would have been very distracting for the children. Children don't seem to mind, and are happily surprised when they come in several days later to see their products on the walls. This activity has the following skill objectives:

2. Language: Beginning Sounds, Name Recognition

3. Computer Literacy: Keyboarding, Desktop Publishing

4. Software utilized: *Superprint* for the Macintosh, Scholastic Software. Or *Superprint II* (Apple II, IBM).

Up Front

TRACKS

As I entered the parking lot, I knew that this was not to be an easy day. The rain was a reminder that there would be no outdoor play. I would have to keep them very busy - especially Jason, who always seemed to have his motor in high gear.

I met with my assistant, Jane, and we went over what we would highlight in the activity centers around the room. We had just completed a unit on dinosaurs, and I wanted to keep the children's interest. To make the transition to a unit on animals, I decided to show how different animals make different tracks in dirt or snow. Jane placed an assortment of rubber animals around the edge of the sand table, while I set up my Apple II. I planned to use the program *Explore-a-Science:Animal Watch:Tracks*. This program was designed for elementary school children, but I felt I could use it to enhance my lesson.

I inserted the program disk and turned on the computer. When instructed, I put in the student disk. As the children arrived, they gathered around the computer to find out what I was doing. I explained that I wanted to tell a story about the picture on the screen. I showed them how we could add characters and words by using the Menu Bar in the top left-hand corner. The children used imagination to help create a quick little story about the scene (footprints in the snow). I printed the story out for the children who helped. Then, as additional children arrived, they helped create a new story based on a new screen.

During our morning circle time, we used our weather guide to indicate the rainy weather outside our window. Randy was still high on dinosaurs, so we discussed some of the things we had learned last week. I then introduced the topic of tracks by asking the children what kinds of tracks the dinosaurs would have made. Jennie told us that her dog had made muddy tracks all over the kitchen when he came in from outside this morning. "Mommy was really mad. Bingo ran and hid under the couch when she started yelling." I asked Jennie if she had seen her dog make the tracks. When she said no, I asked how she knew that it was her dog who made the tracks. Our discussion built from there. I told the children that just as Jennie could tell that her dog had made the tracks in her kitchen, we could also tell what animal had walked through the woods.

From the Menu Bar, I highlighted the picture of the disk and switched to side two of the student disk. I opened up the file called "Deer Tracks." This portion of the program compares the different gaits of two animals. Scene One shows two sets of deer tracks, one made by walking and the other by trotting. In the next screen the children helped me match the deer to its tracks. We talked about how the deer's walk, or gait, affected its tracks. I demonstrated this by moving the animals on the screen. The deer that was walking moved more slowly. We talked about why the deer might be walking and why they might be running. I then opened the file called "Slow Jump." This activity showed the different kinds of tracks a rabbit can make in the snow. The children used problem solving skills while they refined their ability to differentiate. They also were learning the importance of observation and were acquiring a little more information about some animals.

Because the children were getting antsy, I had them pretend to be rabbits and show me how a rabbit would move slowly or quickly. Jason was first, and then led the children around the room in his own version of the bunny hop.

Once we had used up some excess energy, I told the children that we would be making our own tracks. I explained that Jane and I would be calling them up individually. Until they were called, they could "work" in any of the activity centers around the room. I suggested that they might see what kinds of tracks they could make in the sand table, or they might look at some of the new books in the book corner. The art area had all sorts of things with which they could make tracks.

Jane had put a lot of newspaper on the floor and had poured some paint into two aluminum pie plates. These she placed on one end of the run of newspaper. On the other end was a bucket of soapy water and some old towels. We stretched a roll of newsprint between the paint and the soapy water. We had the children come up, one by one, and take off their socks and shoes. They carefully stepped into the pie plates with the paint and then walked across the paper. The result was tracks. Jane wrote the appropriate name on each sheet. We held onto the children as they walked across, as their feet were very slippery from the paint. The children loved it. Some were a little apprehensive at first, but they really got into the project once they felt the paint between their toes.

When everyone had made their own "tracks," we compared them for size, line shape, and even gait (our new word for the day). It was almost time to go home, so Jane and I helped the children get into their raincoats and boots. Jane admitted to me that she had been skeptical when I explained the project, as she doubted that the children would get the gist of the lesson. She now felt that the computer really helped them visualize the different kinds of tracks animals could make. She confessed that she was slowly beginning to recognize the value of the computer for the children.

Teacher Tips:

As we bunny hopped out to meet the parents, I promised the children that we would look for tracks in the play yard if the rain stopped tomorrow. And I promised Jane that she could borrow the computer for the weekend to do some exploring on her own.

Lesson Plan

MAKING NUMBERS MAKE SENSE

Purpose
Students (PreK-K) will solve very simple addition problems, with answers no larger than 5, using pictures and beginning vocabulary.

Materials
Paint With Words, MECC (Apple), *Children's Writing and Publishing Center*, The Learning Co. (Apple, IBM). Paper strips with various number sentences, where the sum is no larger than 5.

Preparation
Prepare word strips for the flannel board, as described below.

Precomputer Activity
Have the children gather together, and show them the *Paint with Words* program. Show them how they can add pictures to their scene, and explain that they are going to try to create a number sentence using pictures. Create a few examples:

2	deer	+	3	deer	=	5	deer
3	frogs	+	1	frog	=	4	frogs

Then talk about what happens when you put together two different characters. What can you call them? You have to come up with a word which would describe them both. Give a few examples.

2	ducks	+	3	fish	=	5	swimmers
1	turtle	+	1	fish	=	2	animals

One way to make this a little more concrete for the children is to use the flannel board, and have them try to put different types of words together into a single category. Some examples of word cards you could use would be the following:

FRUIT:	apples, oranges
PEOPLE:	men, women
BUILDINGS:	houses, farms
WATER ANIMALS:	fish, whales
PETS:	dogs, cats
TOYS:	Barbies, Tonka Trucks

150

Put the categories on one side of the flannel board; the vocabulary words on the other. Call on volunteers to come up and find two vocabulary words which would fit under one category. Have them move them over, until all categories are filled.

Computer Activity

❶ Tell the students that they are going to do the same thing with number sentences. Divide the children into pairs. Give each pair a number sentence (no words, just numbers). Their task is to use the *Paint With Words* program and create a picture showing that number sentence.

❷ Once they have created their picture, they should print it out. When all of the children have finished creating a number sentence picture, have them hold it up in front of the class, and describe what is on their picture, telling the story and showing their number sentence to the others.

❸ Give the children two blank paper strips and have them write their number sentence in two ways, helping them to understand the rule of reciprocation.

Example:
$$2 + 3 = 5$$
$$3 + 2 = 5$$

❹ Lastly, place the pictures on a classroom bulletin board, with the number sentences beneath them.

Follow-Up

If the children are capable of writing short stories (or if you have an adult volunteer who could type a dictated story), have each pair of children go to the computer, and write a short story about their picture, either by hand or using any of the selected children's desktop publishing programs. What do they see in the scene? What is happening? Where are the animals going? etc. The short story can then be added to the bulletin board display.

From The Sidelines

PODD

As we pulled into the parking lot of my son's school, I had to admit that I was a bit curious about this Podd character. For the past week Josh had been saying that Mom and I were going to meet Podd at the school's Open House. Every time we tried to get him to tell us who or what Podd was, he would get an impish look on his face and say, "Wait and see." Well, tonight was the big night.

He led us into his classroom and introduced us to his teacher, Mr. Simon. "Mr. Simon, this is my mom and dad, Mr. Griffith and Mrs. Griffith." We spent the next few minutes looking at the different activity corners in this first grade room. Josh showed us the math table, with blocks neatly stacked, and the science corner equipped with an ant farm. He then pulled us over to the computer area. "This is our computer. We do really neat things on it!"

Before I had a chance to ask him what things, Mr. Simon invited us all to take a seat. He thanked us for coming to Open House. Then he walked around the room, enumerating some of the things the children were learning in each activity area. When he got to the computer area, he pointed out that a puppet stage was next to the computer. He then introduced two fifth graders, Jillian and Robert. He explained that they had been working with the children in experimenting with words. Robert told us that he and Jillian had been helping the children use a computer program called *Podd*. To introduce the children to *Podd*, they had helped each child make his or her own Podd. Jillian then directed our attention to the puppet stage. On cue, a head poked up.

"Hi, my name is Podd and I was made from my Daddy's sock," said a voice that sounded suspiciously like our neighbor's child, Suzy. Podd number 1 disappeared and another Podd appeared. A voice sounding like Josh said, "I'm also Podd. I can do a lot of things. If you name a verb, I will try to do it."

As we heard Jillian's voice say the word *jump*, Podd number 2 disappeared and a third Podd appeared and began to jump. At prompting from Robert or Jillian, each child in the room displayed a "Podd" and had him perform an action verb. We watched 20 different Podd's perform. The last Podd explained, "These are all action verbs." The children were wonderful. Jillian explained that they had made their "Podd" from a sock, adding buttons, wiggly eyes, yarn, and other materials. Each had it's own personality. No two were alike. Robert went on to say that once the children had the hang of action words with the puppet, they moved on to the computer. He and Jillian had taken turns working with two children at a time. Jillian then explained that for the Open House, she had hooked the computer up to a television screen (or large monitor) so that everyone in the room could see the screen. Normally, they just worked in front of the small monitor.

While she was explaining this, Robert had coaxed little Shawna into starting up the computer. The monitor came to life. We were presented with the possibility of two games. Shawna chose number 1 "Find the actions Podd knows."

At the prompting "Podd can -"

Danny, under Jillian's tutelage, typed in the word *jump*. When he hit the RETURN key, Podd began to jump. Next at the computer was Jeff. At the prompt "Podd can - " he typed in the word *run*. Then we got to see Podd run. This was neat.

After a few more demonstrations, Mr. Simon thanked Jillian and Robert and all of the children. He urged us to spend the remaining time looking around the classroom. *Podd* would be at the computer and our children could help us put him to work. The Podd mystery was solved (as well as the mystery of my missing brown sock). When it was our turn to try out the program, I was very impressed. Josh was very at ease using the computer and could even explain the different parts. As he took Podd through his paces, I realized that the computer was helping him to learn through play.

While Josh and his mom went in search of the refreshments, I stopped to chat with Mr. Simon. I told him how impressed I was with the ease with which the children use the computer. He pointed out that they have none of an adult's fears or inhibitions. The computer opens up a new dimension for the children, and he felt that it definitely enhanced his teaching and the children's learning. I congratulated him on an informative Open House and he encouraged me to visit often.

Teacher Response:

The *Podd* program is available from Sunburst/WINGS for learning on both the Apple II and MS-DOS platforms.

Up Front

SORTING BY CATEGORIES

Two of the most important skills that I teach in my early childhood classes are categorization and order. These skills stretches to every part of my students' day - from where to put things when they come in in the morning, to daily routines which require repetitive tasks, to cleaning up at the end of the activity, and on and on. So much of what they learn begins to make more sense when it is put into some kind of order - whether it be word types, history facts, or a recipe. Helping them to practice order and categorization will have life-long benefits.

One way to practice categories which works well (and also serves to introduce them to a "grown-up" word processor) is an activity using *Muppet Slate.*

Muppet Slate is an early childhood word processor, developed using large character sets as well as a full picture dictionary. I had already done some previous work introducing the children to Muppet Slate, and to the concept of a word processor. Muppet Slate's pictures can be incorporated into children's writing at any time with a few easy keystrokes, thus enabling the children to write more through the use of rebus.

The program is easy to use and can substantially enrich any creative writing endeavor. Let me describe an example of how I used this program with my students.

First, I gathered the children in front of the computer, reviewing for them how to move between the text page and the picture dictionary (<CTRL P>). If you have a Muppet Keyboard (an easier, alternative keyboard from Sunburst/WINGS for learning), use it.

Next, I let several children come up to the computer and try going to the dictionary and back. Then I say, "I am thinking of something which starts with the letter 'S'." Once they were comfortable with that, we were ready to start our activity.

I told the children that the purpose of today's task was categorizing. We talked about what categorizing was – putting things in their proper places.

I divided the children into groups of two (more than that in an early learning setting is just too much). Each group was assigned a category.

First, they had to open up a "NEW" file.

Once their file was open, at the top of their page, they were to type in their category. For example:

THINGS THAT MOVE
THINGS IN THE SKY
PEOPLE
ANIMALS ....etc.

I find that even my youngest children can type this much (with or without help) and it is a good way to be introduced to the keyboard (Muppet or regular).

Their next job is to open up the picture dictionary, and go through it, looking for pictures which will fit into their category. If they find a picture that fits, they place it into their document, and go on. If I am working with a particularly bright group of youngsters, I can have them go back at the end, and try typing in the word next to the picture. However, for most of my children, the picture suffices. Once they are done, they can save their document under their names (again - with or without adult help, depending on age).

If there is time in class, I print their work out for them. If not, I do it after class. The next day, all of our category lists are displayed on the bulletin board for all to see and compare. I do assign more than one group the same category. That way, they can compare and see if one group's was identical to the other's - and if not, think about why.

Occasionally, I will change this lesson a little. If, for example, I want to work on values and feelings, I change my categories to subjective ones. For example:

THINGS THAT
MAKE ME WORRY

THINGS THAT
MAKE ME HAPPY

THINGS THAT I
LOVE TO SEE, etc.

Teacher Tips:

1. If the children are of kindergarten age or under, you might want a parent volunteer sitting with them.

2. This lesson can be extended beyond the pictures that are in the *Muppet Slate*. Children can print out their categories, and then cut other pictures out of magazines, and the like to add to their charts.

3. This lesson can work just as well with any program which has a collection of easy clip art for the children. Another example might be *Print Shop*, by Broderbund (available for AppleII , IBM, or Mac), or *Superprint II*, by Scholastic (available for Apple II, IBM, or Mac).

4. SOFTWARE: *Muppet Slate*, Sunburst/WINGS for learning (Apple II)

REFERENCES

1. Author: Charles Hohmann
   Title, Publisher, Date: *Young Children and Computers*. HIGH/SCOPE Press, 1990.
   Strengths: Provides teachers with good practical advice about ways to fit computer use to the developmental stages of young children.
   Drawbacks: Most of the practical activities it describes are for the Apple II series; and much of the software it utilizes has been supplanted by *much* better software

2. Authors: Robert A. DeVillar and Christian J. Faltis,eds.
   Title, Publisher, Date: *Language Minority Students and Computers*. Haworth Press, 1990.
   Strengths: Addresses directly some of the neglected special issues regarding the use of computers with language minority students.
   Drawbacks: The various contributions tend to be more theoretical than practical; some of them seem to buy in too readily to drill and practicy, one on one computer uses.

3. Authors: Steve and Ruth Bennett
   Title, Publisher, Date: *The Official KidPix Activity Book*. Random House Electronic Publishing, 1993.
   Strengths: Provides genuinely creative activities (e.g., Mind Challengers, Bookworks) intended originally for family fun and entertainment, so they can be provided to parents who borrow school computers, as well as adapted by teachers for classroom purposes. In addition, the book illustrates the many ways a creative educator can extend and expand the uses of one piece of software, and "squeeze" the most value out of it.
   Drawbacks: Too many of the activities assume one kid at a time on the computer. Teachers will need to figure out how to adapt the ideas for larger classroom groups.

4. Authors: R. Raskin and C. Ellison
   Title, Publisher, Date: *Parents, Kids, and Computers: An Activity Guide for Family Play and Learning*. Random House Electronic Publishing, 1992.
   Strengths: A good book for teachers to suggest to parents (close to 35% of all families already have computers in the home), and to steal (and adapt) ideas for using good software (*Children's Writing and Publishing, Carmen, KidPix*) in the classroom from.
   Drawbacks: Doesn't sufficiently separate the wheat from the chaff in the software it emphasizes.

5. Author: Anderson, Mary
    Title, Publisher, Date: *Partnerships: Developing Teamwork at the Computer*
    (Majo Press, 1988), 148 pp.
    Strengths: Provides teachers with good practical advice about ways to get
    maximum results from the combination of computers and cooperative
    learning.
    Drawbacks: The software it discusses is getting rapidly out-of date; some of it
    is very drill-and-practicy.

6. Author: Beverly Parker *et al.*
    Title, Publisher, Date: *MicroMath*, Summer, 1993 (v.4, #2). Special Issue
    including "Debate" section on "Children with Special Needs Learning
    Math."
    Strengths: Several articles (including Parker's) help demonstrate how com-
    puters can be *particularly* valuable in supporting the learning of children
    experiencing difficulties with mathematics.
    Drawbacks: Occasionally focuses on issues more relevant in the U.K. than
    the U.S.A.

7. Authors: Susan Ellis and Susan Leyland
    Title, Publisher, Date: *Cooperative Learning: Getting Started.* Scholastic, 1990
    Strengths: A short (72pp), simple, prescriptive, and useful handbook for
    getting started in implementing cooperative learning in the classroom,
    including a clear set of first steps (Ch. 3) for teachers who've never used
    cooperative learning before. Nice little bibliography.
    Drawbacks: No specifics on combining the strengths of cooperative learn-
    ing with the strengths of computer integration.

8. Author: Bonnie K. Nastase and Douglas H. Clements
    Title, Publisher, Date: "Motivational and Social Outcomes of Cooperative
    Computer Education Environments,"*Jl of Computing in Childhood Education,*
    1993 (v.4 #1), 15-43.
    Strengths: Describes research that has important implications for the inte-
    gration of computers and cooperative learning at early primary levels.
    Drawbacks: Relies too heavily on LOGO-based ideas and solutions as a con-
    structivist alternative to drill-and-practice approaches too often foisted on
    young children.

9. Author: Douglas H. Clements, Bonnie K. Nastase and Sudha Swaminathan
    Title, Publisher, Date: "Young Children and Computers: Crossroads and
    Directions from Research,"*Young Children,* January, 1993, 56-64.
    Strengths: Supports the potential for using computers for "substantive edu-
    cational innovations consonant with NAEYC guidelines." Extensive
    bibliography
    Drawbacks: No concrete ideas for practitioners.

10. Author: R. E. Yager, S. M. Blunck, and E. T. Nelson
Title, Publisher, Date: "The Use of Computers to Enhance Science Instruction in Pre-School and K-3 Classrooms" *Jl. of Computing in Childhood Education* V.4, #2, 125-136.
Strengths: Describes and evaluates the use of "Constructivist" materials which coincide with current goals for science teaching.
Drawbacks: Emphasis on Iowa Chautauqua Program at expense of the wider variety of choices available.

11. Author: S.W. Haugland
Title, Publisher, Date: "The Effect of Computer Software on Preschool Children's Developmental Gains," *Jl. of Computing in Childhood Education,* V.3, #1, 1993, 15-30.
Strengths: Shows that children who use open-ended software can make significant gains in intelligence, structural knowledge, long-term memory, complex manual dexterity, and self-esteem.
Drawbacks: No concrete ideas for practitioners.

12. Author: Christine Wright and Mari Nomura
Title, Publisher, Date: *From Toys to Computers.* Self-published; distributed by Don Johnston Developmental Equipment, 1991 (Rev.)
Strengths: Provides parents and teachers with good practical advice about ways to adapt toys and computer use to the needs of young children with special needs; has a great resource section
Drawbacks: The first edition came out in the late 1980's, so more and more of the material is getting out of date.

13. Author: Colette Daiute
Title, Publisher, Date: *Writing and Computers.* Addison Wesley, 1985.
Strengths: Exhibits a profound understanding of writing as a process and how to address that process with children. Good theoretical perspective. Good section on "very young" writers.
Drawbacks: Not as helpful on the practical end, with many of the specifics out of date.

14. Author: T. Perl
Title, Publisher, Date: " Manipulatives and the Computer: A Powerful Partnership for Learners of All Ages." *Classroom Computer Learning,* March, 1990. 20-29.
Strengths: Clarifies the ways in which computers and manipulatives can support each other's impact.
Drawbacks: Lacks references to some recent software that can best help students make the connections between the objects they are manipulating and the concepts they are learning.

SOFTWARE LIST

This list includes all the software mentioned in this book. Each listing includes the title of the software and its publisher. If the software is readily available through a discount distributor, we have included the name of one such distributor and its 800 telephone number. Otherwise, we have included the publisher's telephone number. Call the publisher or the distributor to get current information on pricing and machine platform availability.

Animal Watch: Tracks.
William K. Bradford (800-421-2009)

Balancing Bear
Sunburst/WINGS for learning
(800-321-7511)

Banner Books: Your School Day
Toucan Software
Educational Resources (800-624-2926)

Berenstain Bears
Compton's New Media
Educational Resources (800-624-2926)

Big Book Maker
Toucan Software
Educational Resources (800-624-2926)

Children's Writing and Publishing Center
The Learning Co.
Educational Resources (800-624-2926)

Clifford Software
Scholastic, Inc. (800-541-5513)

Cotton Tales
MindPlay (800-221-7911)

Counting Critters
MECC (800-685-6322)

Explore-a-Science: Tyrannosaurus Rex
William K. Bradford (800-421-2009)

Facemaker
Queue, Inc.
Educational Resources (800-624-2926)

Hop to It
Sunburst/WINGS for learning
(800-321-7511)

Just Grandma and Me
Brøderbund
Learning Services (800-877-9378)

Katie's Farm
Lawrence Productions (800-421-4157)

Kid Pix
Brøderbund
Learning Services (800-877-9378)

Kid Works 2
Davidson and Associates
Educational Resources (800-624-2926)

Learn About Animals
Sunburst/WINGS for learning
(800-321-7511)

McGee, McGee at the Fun Fair
Lawrence Productions (800-421-4157)

Mosaic Magic
Kindermagic Software
Educational Resources (800-624-2926)

Muppet Math
Sunburst/WINGS for learning
(800-321-7511)

Muppet Slate
Sunburst/WINGS for learning
(800-321-7511)

Muppets on Stage
Sunburst/WINGS for learning
(800-321-7511)

Mystery Objects
MECC (800-685-6322)

Once Upon a Time
Compu-Teach
Educational Resources (800-624-2926)

Patterns and Sequences
Hartley Software
Educational Resources (800-624-2926)

Patterns
MECC (800-685-6322)

Paint With Words,
MECC (800-685-6322)

The Playroom
Brøderbund
Educational Resources (800-624-2926)

Podd
Sunburst/WINGS for learning
(800-321-7511)

Print Shop & Printshop Companion
Brøderbund
Learning Services (800-877-9378)

Rosie the Counting Rabbit
William K. Bradford (800-421-2009)

Seasons and Special Days
Sunburst/WINGS for learning
(800-321-7511)

Silly, Noisy House
Voyager
Educational Resources (800-624-2926)

Snoopy Writer
Random House

Stgories & More
IBM/EduQuest (800-793-5327)

Storybook Theater
Sunburst/WINGS for learning
(800-321-7511)

Superprint/Superprint II
Scholastic, Inc. (800-541-5513)

Super Science Activity Shop
Scholastic, Inc. (800-541-5513)

Tapestry
Jostens Learning (800-548-8372)

Teddy & Iggy
Sunburst/WINGS for learning
(800-321-7511)

Teddy Bear-rels of Fun
DLM
Educational Resources (800-624-2926)

Teddy Bear's Picnic
Sunburst/WINGS for learning
(800-321-7511)

Timeliner
Tom Snyder Productions (800-342-0236)

Treehouse
Brøderbund
Educational Resources (800-624-2926)

Woolly Bounce
MECC (800-685-6322)

GETTING STARTED

Necessary Hardware/IBM

The program disk runs on the IBM PC, XT, or AT and many IBM compatibles with at least one disk drive and a minimum of 640 K of available RAM. The program runs under DOS 3.3 or later.

A printer is optional. The printers supported by the program are:

> all Epson printers and compatibles
> all IBM/ProPrinter printers and compatibles
> HP LaserJet and all compatibles

Your work is saved on a separate data disk or hard drive (with the extension .WRI).

Hard Drive Installation/IBM

If you have a hard drive you may install the program on it and run the program from there, while saving your work on floppies. Boot your machine the way you would normally. After the machine has booted, put the program disk into your floppy drive but do not change drives. From the hard drive prompt (C:>) type:

> A: install A C

To start the program, change directories to LESSPLAN and type **GO** at the prompt.

Floppy Drive Use/IBM

If your machine has two floppy drives and no hard drive, use the A: drive for the program disk, and the B: drive for your data disk. From the A> prompt type **GO**.

Necessary Hardware Macintosh

The program disk runs on the Macintosh with a minimum of 1 megabyte of available RAM. A printer is optional. Insert the program disk. (You may copy its contents onto the hard drive.) Click the program icon.

How to Begin

To begin work, you must first open a file. You can select New File from the File pull-down menu or select Open File if a file is available in the directory that you want to use.

Once you have a file open, you can enter and edit text in it. You can save your writing at any time. You can name and close the file and then open any other file that you previously made.

HOW TO USE THE WORD PROCESSOR

Take a few moments to familiarize yourself with the screen layout of the word processing program by opening a file in which to work. Notice the "menu bar" across the top of the screen.

Choosing from the Pull-down Menu Options

You select guide lessons and other program functions from the pull-down menus on the upper menu bar. Menu options that are grayed out are inactive. Shortcut keys are listed next to some menu options. Prompts for carrying out functions appear at the bottom of the screen (MS-DOS version).

MS-DOS MENUS

Help Menu

About Program gives information about the publisher and developer of the program.

Help (<F1>) is available from any part of the word processing program. When you access a Help Screen, you are really looking at one page in the Help Book. Use <PgUp/PgDn> to move back and forth in the Help Book.

Screen Display (Alt-S) allows you to customize the screen colors. Use the arrow keys to choose what you want changed and the <+> and <-> keys to change colors.

Data Path (Alt-D) allows you to change where the program will look for the data disk, referred to as the "default" data drive. Ordinarily this will be drive C. It displays the current drive and prompts you to enter the letter of the drive and the path where you want your work saved.

You cannot change drives while a file is open.

File Menu

The File Menu enables you to end your work in a file, as well as do other things such as printing and saving your files.

New File (<F8>) begins a new file. Enter a file name (up to 8 characters). Then begin work.

Open File (<F4>) opens any file that was created with this software and saved on your data disk. To open a file, select *Open File* (when no file is open), highlight a file name from the list that appears, and press <Enter>.

Close File (<F9>) closes a file when you want to stop working on it. To save changes you have made to a file without replacing the original file, choose *Save File;* then when you are asked if you want to use the same name, press N for No, and type in a new name for the file into the prompt area; then press <Enter>.

Insert File (<F7>) puts a file that has been made with this software into your open file. Put the cursor where the file is to be inserted, select *Insert File*, and in the prompt area enter the name of the file you want to insert.

Save File (<F3>) saves an open file in its present version and allows you to continue working on it.

Save as ASCII saves a copy of the open file in ASCII format. When a file is saved as an ASCII file, the program can not open it. The file is stripped of all special formatting. This is useful if you want to use a copy of your work with a different word processing program that can open ASCII files. The ASCII files have a file name extension of .ASC.

Print Options (<F6>) sets the printing options. Default values shown in the right-hand column below. They may be changed, within the limits in parentheses in the middle column. The program does not allow you to use numbers outside those limits. Options remain as set until you change them again or until you reload the program.

Title	FILENAME	
Left Margin	(1 - 65)	7
Right Margin	(10 - 79)	75
Line Spacing	(1 - 3)	1
Top Line	(1 - 60)	7
Bottom Line	(7 - 90)	60
Paper Length	(6 - 90)	66
Stop between Pages	(Y or N)	N
Page Numbering	(Y or N)	Y
Laser Printer	(Y or N)	N

Change "Stop between Pages" to Y for Yes if you intend to feed paper by hand. If the line spacing does not come out as you expected, check your printer manual for setup routines.

Print File (<F5>) prints the file you are working on using the Print Options as above or as you have set them. You may choose to print **All** the pages of your file or you may choose a **from** and **to** page range. Use the arrow keys to move the highlight.

Copy File duplicates a file that you choose from your data disk and puts the duplicate on the same data disk. To copy a file, select the file and type in the new file name for the copy; then press <Enter>.

Rename File enables you to give a new name to any file on your data disk. To rename a file, select the file and type in the new file name; then press <Enter>.

Erase File deletes files made with this program.

Quit closes the file you have open and quits the program.

Edit Menu

Undo (Alt-U) cancels the last Cut or Paste Text command. (You cannot undo other commands.) You can use the Undo function only immediately after you've cut or pasted text and before pressing any other keys.

Mark Text (Alt-M) allows you to mark a part of your document and then use Edit Menu and/or Format Menu functions on the marked text. Select Mark Text, then follow the instructions in the prompt area to highlight the text to mark. Then use <F2> to pull down a menu and select; or use the shortcut keys.

Cut Text (Alt-K) allows you to delete a marked part of your document. Select Cut Text after you have used Mark Text.

Copy Text (Alt-C) duplicates a part of your document. Select Copy Text after you have used Mark Text. The marked text is copied into the computer's memory until Alt-C or Alt-K is used again. Move the cursor to the place to insert the copy and Paste Text (see below).

Paste Text (Alt-P) pastes into your document a copy of text that you have marked and cut or copied. After you have used Cut or Copy Text, move the cursor to the place to insert the copy and select Paste Text. A copy of the text will appear in the new place.

Overstrike (<INS>) allows you to switch between Insert and Overstrike text entry mode. The bottom right corner of the screen indicates which text entry mode is active.

Find Menu

Find enables you to instruct the program to locate every occurrence of a "string" of characters. Choose *Find* from the Find Menu, then in the prompt area type in the "string," and then press <Enter>. *Find* starts at the cursor, loops through the end of the file and back to the cursor position until every instance of the string is found. Press <ESC> to cancel *Find*.

Replace replaces strings of characters. Choose *Replace* from the Find Menu, then type in the characters and spaces that you want to replace in the prompt area, then press <Enter>. Then type exactly what you want used instead and press <Enter>. (Although the *Find* function ignores upper and lower case, the replacement will use the upper and lower case characters exactly as you specify). Each time the string is found, the program asks if you want to replace it. <ESC> stops the *Replace* command but leaves all the changes already made.

Format Menu

Functions on the Format Menu determine how your work will appear on screen and in print.

Underline (Ctrl-U) Use this command immediately after you have used Mark Text (see above) to mark characters you want underlined. On the screen, the underlined text shows up as a different color.

Bold (Ctrl-B) Use this command immediately after you have used Mark Text (see above) to mark characters you want to appear in boldface. On the screen, the boldfaced text shows up as a different color.

Plain (Ctrl-P) Use this command immediately after you have used Mark Text (see above) to mark characters you want to appear in plain text. Plain removes Underline, Bold, Center, and Quote formatting.

Center (Ctrl-C) Use this command immediately after you have used Mark Text (see above) to mark characters you want to appear centered in your file. On the screen, everything will be centered until the next carriage return.

Quote (Ctrl-Q) Use this command immediately after you have used Mark Text (see above) to mark characters that are direct quotations and that you want to appear in your file indented and single spaced on the printed page. On the screen, any blocks of text formatted by Quote will be indented and single spaced.

Adjust Margins (Ctrl-J) Use this command immediately after you have used Mark Text (see above) to mark characters that you want to give special margins. Margins set with Ctrl-J override the margins set with Print Options. Each time you use this command, you are asked to enter the Left and Right Indent that you want. The adjusted margins remain in effect until the program encounters a carriage return in your text.

Line Spacing (Ctrl-S) sets line spacing (1>, 2>, or 3>). Mark the text you want to have special Line Spacing and then select Line Spacing from the Format Menu. You are then asked to type 1 for single spacing, 2 for double spacing, or 3 for triple spacing.

The spacing remains as set until the next carriage return. This command is useful when you want to change the line spacing for part of a document.

New Page (Ctrl-N) starts a new page. An N is displayed in the left margin with a dotted line and the Page Number, and the cursor moves to the next line to show where the inserted page is.

Guide Menu

To do the guide lessons, choose one listed in the Guide Menu. Whenever you choose a guide lesson, the computer screen splits horizontally, with the guide lesson that you chose appearing in the bottom part of the screen. Your working area (text entry area) remains at the top. You can still write in the text area and use the pull-down menus and help functions.

Each guide contains a number of "pages" on instruction. The prompt area tells you where you are in the lesson (example, "Page 3 of 9") as well as the commands to go forward <Ctrl-G> and to go backward <Ctrl-T>.

When an guide lesson is open, you can switch back to the full screen to write by pressing <ESC>. If you re-select that guide lesson from the Guide Menu, the program remembers where you were and picks up right where you left off.

Exit Guide when you have finished with a guide lesson, or to switch back to the full screen for writing. To switch back and forth between two guide lessons when you have one displayed already, just select the other from the menu. It will appear in the Guide window at the bottom of the screen. When you re-select the previous guide lesson, it will pick up just where you left off.

Practice Menu

Making a selection from the Practice Menu copies text into the open file so you can use the word processor to edit it. Any changes that you make in your file do not change the text items on this menu.

Usually instructions in a guide lesson you have chosen from the Guide Menu will tell you when to use a practice file. Once you are familiar with them, you may want to select them to use on your own whenever you want.

Notes Menu

The Notes Menu opens a database file of "records." You may not type in your file while the Notes options are in use.

View opens the file for browsing. If a record is too large to fit in the area at the bottom of the screen, use the Up and Down <ARROWS> to scroll the record. To move from one record to the next use the <PgUp> and <PgDn> keys. Pressing <ESC> closes the file.

Edit opens the database file with your cursor in it to enable you to edit records. Use the <ARROWS> to move the cursor in the record. Whatever you type will be entered at the cursor. The total amount allowed in each file is as follows:

Materials	100
Objectives	120
Activity	715
Grade level	10
Topic or Skills	60
Class/Group/Pair Activity	16

The <INS> key toggles between insert and overstrike mode. <Delete> and <backspace> enable you to erase. To move from one record to the next use <PgUp> and <PgDn>. Pressing <ESC> closes the file. Your changes are kept in the computer's memory until you save the Notes file or exit the program. To add a blank record to the database use <Ctrl-R> from the Edit record screen.

Find lets you select specific records by finding those that have a common element that you ask the program to look for. Choose *Find* from the Notes Menu, then press <Enter>. Type into the appropriate field the characters that you want the program to search for. Press <Ctrl-X> when you want to begin the search. *Find* will make active only those records that contain characters to match what you typed in. When the search is completed, the status line at the bottom of the screen will tell you how many records are active. When *Find* is used again, it will search through only the active records. With each new search, you are working with successively smaller and smaller subsets of the database file, until you press <Ctrl-A> to return to all records for a brand new search.

Copy enables you to mark a part of a record and put it into your open file, where you may use the word processor to edit it. Use View or Find to display the record you want to copy from, then select *Copy* from the Notes Menu. The cursor will appear in the record. Follow the instructions in the prompt area to *Mark* and *Copy* what you want. The cursor will then appear in your writing file. Move it to the place where you want to insert the copy and press <Enter>.

Special Keys

Special function keys available in the word processing program.

<F1>	Help	<F6>	Print Options
<F2>	Menu	<F7>	Insert File
<F3>	Save File	<F8>	New File
<F4>	Open File	<F9>	Close File
<F5>	Print File	<F10>	Quit

Special short cut commands in the word processing program.

<Alt-U>	Undo
<Ctrl-U>	Underline
<Alt-M>	Mark Text
<Ctrl-B>	Boldface
<Alt-K>	Cut Text
<Ctrl-P>	Plain
<Alt-C>	Copy Text
<Ctrl-C>	Center
<Alt-P>	Paste Text
<Ctrl-Q>	Quote
<Alt-F>	Find
<Ctrl-J>	Adjust Margins
<Alt-R>	Replace
<Ctrl-S>	Line Spacing
<Alt-S>	Screen Display
<Ctrl-N>	New Page
<Alt-D>	Set Data Path

<ESC>	cancel a command, back out of a screen
<ARROWS>	move the cursor
<BACKSPACE>	erase backward (to the left of the cursor)
<DEL>	erase forward (erase the cursor character or space)
<INS>	change between INSERT and OVERSTRIKE

MACINTOSH MENUS

File Menu
(See section under MS-DOS Menus.)

Save as... renames the open file and saves it with a new name.

You may choose to save the file in Normal or Text File Format. The program can only open files saved in Normal File Format.

Page Setup... and **Page Margins...** determines how your document will be printed. See your printer manual for information regarding the Page Setup dialog box. Page Margins have been set for normal 8 1/2" by 11" page printing. You may change any or all of the four margins (top, bottom, left, and right). You may also set the starting page number.

Show by Page displays a small facsimile of your document.

Print... (⌘ P) enables you to print your work. For information about the options in the dialog box, refer to your printer manual.

Edit Menu

(See section under MS-DOS Menus. Note: Mark Text in standard Macintosh way, that is, click and drag.)

Clear deletes marked text.

Select All (⌘ A) marks your entire document. Whatever function you then choose will affect the entire contents.

Find/Replace (⌘ F) lets you find a string of characters or find and replace a string with another string.

Find Next (⌘ N) takes you to the next occurrence of the string you have specified.

Show/Hide Ruler and **Show/Hide ¶** are "toggles" that reveal information about the format of your page. Click *Show Ruler* if you want to display a ruler across the top of the screen. You can then see where the line length is set and where you have placed any Tabs. (Leaving it turned off gives you a little more on-screen space for writing.)

Font Menu

The Font Menu allows you to select any of the fonts for your documents.

Style Menu

This menu allows you to select type styles and sizes for what you write in the program.

Format Menu

Line Spacing allows you to change the default width of space between lines. Enter the spacing you want in the dialog box. To return to the default spacing, enter the number 0 in the dialog box. If you place the cursor at the beginning of a new line and then change the line spacing, the line spacing you specify will remain in effect as you enter text until you change it back.

Set Tab allows you to set your tabs. When you click this function, the ruler is displayed with a small pointer as your cursor. Use the mouse to put the pointer at the position on the ruler where you want to set the tab. Once a tab has been set, you can move it to other positions; use the mouse to activate the pointer and then drag it to its new location on the ruler. To delete it alto-gether, drag it into the writing area.

Align Left, **Align Right**, **Center**, and **Justify** options enable you to set the placement of text on the page. This function affects the entire paragraph where your cursor is. Normally text is left-justified (the default setting), which means it lines up along the left margin. If you want to change the placement of a paragraph, select the paragraph that you want changed by clicking in it; then select *Align Right*, *Center*, or *Justify* from the Format Menu. Highlighting text in more than one paragraph will cause the func-tion to affect each paragraph.

Open Header and **Open Foote**r allow you to put page numbers (or other text) at the top and/or bottom of each page of your printed text. Click on either of these options and enter the text you want to have printed. The paragraph symbol indicates a carriage return has already been entered. Enter your text in front of that carriage return. You can enter additional carriage returns by pressing Return.

To have the printer number your pages, select *Insert Page Number* after you have chosen *Open Header* or *Open Footer*. If you want the page number centered, use the *Center* option on the Format Menu.

Guide Menu
(See section under MS-DOS Menus.)

If the guide lesson will not fit in the guide display area, the scroll bar to the right is active and "(scroll)" appears at the bottom of the window. Use the mouse to switch the active scroll bar between the guide area and the text entry area.

Practice Menu
(See section under MS-DOS Menus.)

Notes Menu
(See section under MS-DOS Menus.)

View\Edit (⌘ J) opens a database of notecard records. If a record is too large to fit in the area at the bottom of the screen, the scroll bar next to the record is available. To move from one notecard to the next, use the Next and Previous buttons in the prompt line or *Next Record* and *Previous Record* from the Notes Menu. Clicking the Exit button or selecting *Exit Notes* from the Notes Menu closes the database file.

To edit a notecard in the database, select *View\Edit* from the Notes Menu and move to the notecard you want to edit by clicking the Next or Previous buttons. Double-click below the "field name." The field expands to fill the bottom area and your cursor is active there. Whatever you type will be entered at the cursor. When you have finished editing any field and want to keep the changes, click the Done button. Click the Cancel button to exit the "Edit mode" without saving your work on the notecard.

Find Notes (⌘ K) opens a dialog box for you to type into the appropriate field the sequence of letters that you want the program to search for. Click the Begin Search button when you want to begin the search.

When the search is completed, a dialog box appears which tells you how many records are active. To return to all the records for a brand new search, click the All button or select *All Records* from the Notes Menu.

Copy Notes (⌘ L) allows you to copy text from all fields of a record and paste it into your file. First, display the record that you want to copy from. Then select *Copy Notes*. The cursor will appear in the record. Use the mouse to highlight the part of the notecard that you want. Then select *Copy* from the Edit Menu. Put your cursor into your writing file where you want the notecard; then select *Paste* from the Edit Menu. The database file remains in "Copy Notes mode" until you click the Next or Previous button.

If you have edited the notecard presently displayed, a dialog box will appear and ask if you want to save. Click the Yes button to save the current version of the notecard.

Next Record (⌘])/**Previous Record** (⌘ [ ) moves through the Notes database one record at a time.

Add Record (⌘ D) adds an empty record to the end of the database. You may then enter text and edit the record using the "Edit mode" of *View/Edit*.

All Records undoes any Find Notes searches and makes all the records active.

Exit Notes closes the Notes display area. If you have edited the notecard displayed, a dialog box will offer you the opportunity to save it. If there was a guide lesson open before the Notes option was used, that guide reappears.

Special Keys

Listed below are special function keys available in the word processing program. Menus show the shortcut keys.

(⌘ O)	Open...	(⌘ T)	Plain Text
(⌘ W)	Close	(⌘ B)	Bold
(⌘ S)	Save	(⌘ I)	Italics
(⌘ P)	Print...	(⌘ U)	Underline
(⌘ Q)	Quit	(⌘ G)	Next Page
(⌘ Z)	Undo	(⌘ R)	Previous Page
(⌘ X)	Cut	(⌘ E)	Exit Guide
(⌘ C)	Copy	(⌘ J)	View
(⌘ V)	Paste	(⌘ K)	Find Notes
(⌘ A)	Select All	(⌘ L)	Copy Notes
(⌘ F)	Find/Replace	(⌘])	Next Record
(⌘ N)	Find Next	(⌘ [ )	Previous Record
		(⌘ D)	Add Record

<ESC>	cancel a command, back out of a screen
<ARROWS>	move the cursor
<DELETE>	erase backward (to the left of the cursor)